HEA
CONFLICT,
PEACEFUL
LIFE

A BIBLICAL GUIDE FOR COMMUNICATING
THOUGHTS, FEELINGS, AND OPINIONS
WITH GRACE, TRUTH, AND ZERO REGRET

DONNA JONES

NELSON
BOOKS

An Imprint of Thomas Nelson

Healthy Conflict, Peaceful Life

Published in Nashville, Tennessee, by Nelson Books, an imprint of Thomas Nelson. Nelson Books and Thomas Nelson are registered trademarks of HarperCollins Christian Publishing, Inc.

Published in association with COMPEL, a writers community founded by Lysa TerKeurst.

Published in association with the literary agency of Brock, Inc., P.O. Box 384, Matthews, NC 28105.

Thomas Nelson titles may be purchased in bulk for educational, business, fundraising, or sales promotional use. For information, please email SpecialMarkets@ThomasNelson.com.

Library of Congress Cataloging-in-Publication Data

Names: Jones, Donna, 1961- author.
Title: Healthy conflict, peaceful life : a biblical guide for communicating thoughts, feelings, and opinions with grace, truth, and zero regret / Donna Jones.
Description: Nashville, Tennessee : Nelson Books, [2024] | Summary: "Author, speaker, and pastor's wife Donna Jones gives women a practical, biblical blueprint for making regret-free choices in the middle of real-life conflict so they can exchange relational turmoil for personal and relational peace"-- Provided by publisher.
Identifiers: LCCN 2023037949 (print) | LCCN 2023037950 (ebook) | ISBN 9781400243990 (trade paperback) | ISBN 9781400243716 (ebook)
Subjects: LCSH: Conflict management--Religious aspects--Christianity. | Interpersonal relations--Religious aspects--Christianity. | Communication--Religious aspects--Christianity. | Christian life.
Classification: LCC BV4597.53.C58 J655 2024 (print) | LCC BV4597.53.C58 (ebook) | DDC 248.8/6--dc23/eng/20231012
LC record available at https://lccn.loc.gov/2023037949
LC ebook record available at https://lccn.loc.gov/2023037950

Printed in the United States of America

23 24 25 26 27 LBC 5 4 3 2 1

To my parents, who showed me how loving families handle conflict with grace, truth, forgiveness, and a whole lot of laughter.

To my husband, my pastor, and the best man I know, JP Jones. Thank you for loving me well, especially during the early years as we struggled to figure out how to handle conflict without regret. You taught me wisdom and humility, and you fill my life with joy. When I got you, I got the prize!

To my children, Taylor, Kylie, and Ashton. You are my greatest gifts from God. I didn't always process conflict well, but I tried to always apologize when I didn't. What we didn't have in the way of perfection, we made up for in an abundance of love and grace. Which, when I think about it, is the beautiful message of the gospel.

I couldn't love you all more.

CONTENTS

CONTENTS

INTRODUCTION

We've never met, but I know you.

If I asked you about your deepest joy, you'd smile and tell me about a relationship, wouldn't you? A child. A spouse. A parent. A friend.

But if I asked you about your deepest heartache, you'd also tell me about a relationship. Am I right?

A falling-out with a family member, hurt from a friend, or conflict with a colleague leaves us reeling, wondering what to do about it. We replay the event in the shower. We rehash it with our friends. We can't eat—or we can't stop eating. We can't sleep—or we can't stop sleeping.

We rehearse conversations in our cars, obsessing over what he said. What she said. What we said.

What we *wished* we'd said.

Conflict consumes us in all its forms. Sure, we smile and function on the outside. We go to work. Take the kids to school. Call our moms. Celebrate holidays. But on the inside, we're miserable. We're confused. We're ashamed. We're angry. We're wounded. We're guilt-ridden. We're hopeless.

We're hurt.

Conflict never slips into our lives on her own; her friends—heartache, headaches, and hurt—always tag along. These companions don't make good party guests; they make painful ones.

But you already know this. That's why you picked up this book.

Maybe you can recall the exact moment you knew you needed wisdom for a relationship conflict.

Sometimes it happens in a flash: a text, a blowup, a breakup, or a phone call sends us into a tailspin. Other times, though, relationships fizzle and fade like the embers of a day-old fire. The friend you thought would always have your back starts snubbing you instead; the spouse you thought you'd always feel close to now seems like a stranger; the toddler you thought would never rebel grows into a teenager causing never-ending drama.

You wake up one day and everything seems manageable. You wake up the next day and realize it's not.

So what do you do when you're standing in your kitchen with an upset teenager? How do you work through real-time disagreements with your spouse? What's the best response when you're blindsided by a text from a disgruntled coworker? What should you say to a family member who has strong political opinions that run counter to yours? How do you broach the subject with a friend who hurt your feelings?

This is the stuff life is made of.

What we do in the midst of this stuff will leave us holding either a bouquet of relief or a fistful of regret.

None of us wants to hang our head in shame and think, *Why did I handle the conflict like that?*

The good news—the *great* news, actually—is that it's possible to take hurtful conflicts and turn them into holy moments that God can use to work in us and through us.

In the pages of this book we'll explore a practical, biblical blueprint for resolving conflict and genuinely connecting with others. We'll learn how to honor God when we've been hurt, how to communicate when we'd rather retaliate, and how to move toward others when it seems easier to run away. We'll discuss why conflict happens, what to do in the heat of conflict, and what to do to prevent conflict. You'll walk away with a clear understanding of how to respond when conflict comes calling.

Whether you deal with daily disagreements or occasional blowups, *Healthy Conflict, Peaceful Life* will show you how to communicate your thoughts, feelings, and opinions with grace, truth, and zero regret.

ONE

THE DAY I WANTED TO BURN DOWN THE CHURCH

I wiped my tears and blew my nose before I picked up the phone to dial. As I waited for my friend to answer, I glanced into my rearview mirror. Puffy lids and bloodshot eyes stared back at me. *Lovely. Just lovely,* I thought. My oversized sunglasses would have to remain glued to my face if my friend could free herself long enough to meet me for lunch.

How had it come to *this*?

After seven years pastoring a small church, my husband was offered a dream job as the teaching pastor at a large, flourishing church in California. Because JP hadn't sought this job out, we felt confident the offer was straight from the hand of God. With anticipation of great things to come, we packed up our house, piled our three kids in the car, and headed for the promised land.

And for us, it was indeed the promised land.

The church staff was warm and friendly, the people were receptive, and the ministry was fulfilling. People came to Christ in such numbers we almost lost count. I began teaching a weekly Bible study that grew from seventy-five women to three hundred women in three years. Our whole family thrived.

Then, seven years into our dream job, the senior pastor decided to retire. What happened next is almost too ugly to recount on paper. Factions developed. People jockeyed for power. JP and I (and others) endured a near-yearlong journey into hell. At the request of my husband, I attended one particularly pivotal elder board meeting. This was new terrain for me. I assumed we'd pray and worship and that the elder board would calmly discuss issues at hand. Instead, JP and I sat stunned, mouths ajar, as leaders lied, distorted, and manipulated. No voices were raised, but the punches leveled in that room were as barbaric as a bar fight.

This was conflict on steroids.

And we were caught in the middle.

It was all so hurtful. And hard. And confusing. How could conflict among Christians escalate to the point of destroying long-time friendships, families, and our church community? Desperate to handle the conflict in a Christ-honoring way, I managed to keep a semi-clear head and Spirit-filled attitude.

Until the lies hit home.

In an unexpected turn of events, my husband became the target, not for everyone, but for some.

I cried more tears that year than all other years before or since, combined. Some days the conflict-induced heartache became so overwhelming I drove my SUV around the corner, parked in front of my neighbor's lot, and sobbed—wailed, actually—until I could pull myself together enough to care for our kids without crying.

I didn't want our conflict to become my children's commentary on how Christians should treat one another.

Of course, you can't hide things from kids. They knew. But I think they also knew we remained committed to honoring Christ in the way we tried to handle the conflict. We didn't respond in kind. We didn't gossip or slander, although more than once I wanted to. We did our best to forgive, or more honestly, we did our best to *want* to forgive.

That is, until the day I snapped.

The disagreements, disappointment, and disillusionment in how people *should* act versus how they *did* act reached a boiling point. I was sick of the conflict and fed up with the turmoil. Hurt turned to anger. Anger turned to rage. It all felt so unfair, and I just wanted the whole thing to stop.

But how?

A lunch with my best friend would surely pull me out of my funk. I blew my nose again and dialed her number, hopeful her presence would provide relief from the heartache and hurt. I could hardly wait to spill all my pent-up frustration.

At noon I wheeled into the parking lot where Julie greeted me with a big hug. We walked arm in arm into our favorite restaurant, found an uncrowded spot, and ordered quickly. When we were finally sure we wouldn't be interrupted or overheard, Julie's eyes met mine.

"How are you doing?"

I leaned forward with barely enough courage to whisper my private confession: "Some days I feel like burning the church down."

She looked horrified. I'm certain not even my best friend grasped how deeply the constant conflict, and the energy it took to manage it, had drained me.

"I highly recommend you don't ever repeat that out loud again," she said with a nervous laugh.

She was protecting me, of course, which I loved. Then again, the conflict hadn't been hers. She hadn't lived, breathed, slept, and dreamed conflict for months on end. I had.

Now, before you slam the book shut in horror, wondering how any sane Christian woman (a pastor's wife, at that!) could possibly entertain such a diabolical thought, you should know I was never actually serious about the action, nor do I condone the thought.

But you likely already know that when conflict becomes personal, especially if it involves someone we love like a child or spouse, we're primed to consider anything to stop the pain—even stupid, destructive, ungodly stuff that would only make things worse if carried out and leave us burdened with remorse.

Of course, most of us don't fantasize about burning down a church. (Sorry, Julie, the truth is out.) Perhaps you haven't found yourself in the middle of public conflict, but have you ever been caught up in office politics or cultural criticism? Have you ever felt blindsided by a family feud, a friendship fracture, or a falling-out with a neighbor or coworker? Who among us hasn't (at least, on occasion) allowed other people's sinful behavior to incite our own?

Let's just be honest—conflict hurts, which makes it hard to handle in a holy way.

> LET'S JUST BE HONEST— CONFLICT HURTS, WHICH MAKES IT HARD TO HANDLE IN A HOLY WAY.

Even as you read these words, you might find yourself worn out from marital discord or worn down by parental battles. Given our current cultural climate, you're likely drained by the barrage of discord, disunity, and dissension broadcast on the news and our social media feeds. Every. Single. Day.

Over time, intense conflict can bring out the beast in the best women among us.

Relational chaos affects us more profoundly than any other type of trauma. Eventually the turmoil we feel on the inside spills to the outside, affecting everything and everyone in our way. Discouragement and defeat become our constant companions.

We don't want to yell at our kids, but we're embarrassed to admit that we do. We know the silent treatment doesn't draw us closer to our spouse, but we continue to shut him out. We don't want our friendship to fade into oblivion, but we can't find the courage to address the hurt. We hate the critical, controlling, cynical side of ourselves, but somehow it keeps coming to the surface.

No, we don't dream about burning down buildings, but in our darker moments we dream about getting even or running away. We set fire to our relationships with outbursts, name-calling, silent treatments, and slammed doors. We avoid rather than address. We wield words like weapons, wounding those we love, then watch in horror as our relationships go up in smoke.

Frankly, not many of us know—I mean really *know*—how to handle conflict in a God-honoring, peace-producing, regret-relieving way.

But we want to. Oh, how we desperately want to!

Maybe you've found yourself thinking . . .

I don't know how to stop all the arguing in my home.
I don't know how to break down walls and reconnect.
I don't know how to resolve conflict in a way that restores rather than destroys the relationship.
I don't know how to have the conversation I know I need to have.
I don't know how to tell others what I need without feeling guilty or appearing bossy.

*I don't know how to avoid getting sucked into family/office/
friend/social media drama.*
*I don't know how to express my opinions without getting into
an argument.*
I don't know how to make this relationship better.

If you've ever found yourself thinking these thoughts—or
thoughts like them—you've come to the right place.

———o———

Generally our relationships clip along well, but occasionally—
bam!—a friend hurts our feelings, our husband disappoints, our
child makes a really bad decision, our family dynamics fill with
drama, or our church faces a crisis. We're left sucker punched, barely
able to breathe, standing with fists full of broken dreams, wondering
how to put our relationships back together. To complicate matters,
an ever-increasing number of us have grown up in families of origin who failed to hand us tools for handling hurt, calming chaos,
building bridges, inspiring trust, working through conflict, or
communicating in ways that draw others in rather than shut them
down. As a result, we struggle to confidently navigate the ups and
downs of human relationships, especially when conflict rears its
ugly head. At best, we end up with relational hiccups or headaches,
but at worst, we end up hurt or heartbroken.

We don't want hurt. We don't want heartbreak. And if we are
being completely honest, we don't even want headaches or hiccups.

We want peace. We *need* peace.

And we want our peace spilling out onto those around
us—creating strong marriages, close friendships, and loving,

respectful relationships with our kids, parents, siblings, coworkers, and community.

We are Christians; we want to *live* like Christians, even in the midst of conflict. Maybe *especially* in the midst of conflict, because that's where it matters most.

This is what we want. We know it in our bones. The problem is we don't always know how to make it happen.

What we *do* know is that we're tired of screaming matches and silent treatments. We're sick of conflict and chaos. We're desperate to find a way out of our disconnection, disappointment, and discontentment. We're over misunderstanding and being misunderstood. We know there must be a better way. We know God says there is.

But entire generations of men and women—maybe you're one of them—feel ill-equipped to have the kinds of relationships they want, largely because they never learned how to successfully navigate inevitable human conflict.

Unless someone tells them.

I'm about to tell you.

The truths within these pages have been hard-fought for me to learn. Candidly, I'm still learning (just ask the people who know me!), but I'm committed to living out my faith by handling human conflict according to God's blueprint. When faced with disagreements, misunderstandings, or differences of opinion, I don't want to say or do things I'll look back on with remorse. I'm guessing you can relate.

Do we want peace? Definitely. Do we long for resolution and reconciliation? Of course. But more than these things, we need wisdom to handle conflict without regret.

I suspect these lessons will be hard-fought for you, too, largely because the very conflict-induced headaches, heartaches, and hurt we try so hard to avoid are the same tools God places in our hands to help us build better and more beautiful ways of relating to others.

Make no mistake: God *has* given us the tools we need. It's up to us to learn what they are and how to use them.

WHERE DO WE START?

During our tumultuous season dealing with church conflict, had you peeled back my perfectly curated outer layer and peeked into my inner soul, you would have seen the circus lady on the tightrope—the one who makes you cringe because she looks so close to toppling off you fear she might perish. Looking back, I did a masterful job of hiding my pain and confusion. I gave the illusion of knowing how to manage the internal chaos caused by the external conflict. And, to some degree, I did know what to do. (Thank God for the instructions found in His Word!) Even so, I still had much to learn about how to handle conflict so the end result is peace without regret.

May I cut to the chase and tell you the biggest mistake I made during that season of my life? It's probably not what you'd expect.

Here it is: I wanted other people to change.

After all, the conflict was because of *them*, right?

Who hasn't said "If only so-and-so would change, the relationship would be better"? Frankly, some relationships *would* be better if the other person changed.

But, try as we might, we can't change others. We can only change ourselves.

Honestly, writing these words—*we can't change others*—feels a bit defeating. Unfair, even. Why should I have to change when the problem isn't me? I *want* others to change. I beg God to make others change. I feel frustrated when He doesn't answer my prayer and *make* them change. What's up with that? They *should* change! They'd be better, we'd be better, *everything* would be better if only they'd change.

They wouldn't even have to change a lot. I'm not talking about full personality overhauls. I'm talking about little adjustments. Little tweaks. Little shifts.

Because if *they* would change, *I* wouldn't have to. And wow, that sounds like a great game plan to me.

I'm guessing you can relate.

Years ago I was speeding down the freeway praying for one of my then-preteen daughters. At the time, we butted heads on nearly everything, though it hadn't been that way when she was younger. I prayed, *Lord, I'm worn out from constant conflict. Please change her.*

God's answer was as clear as if He were sitting in my passenger seat: *You are praying the wrong prayer. I don't need to change her personality; I need to change your perspective on her personality.*

Indeed, He did.

Still, life would be so much easier if those around us would think like us, believe like us, live like us, and love like us. If they would anticipate our needs, accommodate our desires, and acquiesce to our decisions, we could skip through life conflict-free. *Cue the confetti!*

This isn't how relationships work though.

We cannot change someone else. We can only change ourselves.

Ironically, and maybe mercifully, this truth is often most evident to those of us who are in relationships with the most difficult people, the ones we deem unchangeable. But give us a relationship that's halfway normal, and we go to town trying to fix, control, alter, adjust, convince, manipulate, and correct. *After all*, we reason, *if they could just be a bit more responsive, a little more understanding—if only they were different in this way, or that way—they wouldn't grate on us like sandpaper on wood. Instead, we'd float through life like the lingering scent of perfume. Lovely.*

But here's where the desire for other people to change becomes problematic: if we believe we can't handle conflict well unless someone else changes, we relinquish our right to our own relational well-being. Essentially, we hand our spiritual and emotional peace over to our spouse, child, friend, coworker, boss, or neighbor, who may or may not change.

I cannot give the key to my peace to someone who is not relationally healthy. Actually, I can't give it to anyone. The key to spiritual and relational peace is mine.

> I AM NOT RESPONSIBLE FOR HOW SOMEONE ELSE HANDLES CONFLICT. I AM ONLY RESPONSIBLE FOR HOW I HANDLE CONFLICT.

I am not responsible for how someone else handles conflict. I am only responsible for how I handle conflict.

The hard truth is that I cannot make another person choose to relate like God wants people to relate, especially in the midst of disagreements and dissension. However, I do have a choice when it comes to how *I* relate and respond. I can surrender myself to doing things God's way, living in dependence on His power, or I can dig in my heels and do things my way, with an unhealthy obsession over other people's behavior. This simple shift in focus—my choices in conflict, not their choices in conflict—was a game changer for me.

Was this easy? Not always.

As I've already admitted, I wanted other people to stop being difficult. My thought process went something like this: *Could you please just be easy to love so I don't have to adjust my way of thinking/ doing/living to accommodate you? I don't want to make the choice to handle conflict well. I don't even want to* think *about choices or conflict. I want to effortlessly glide through life without a speck of emotional toil. And if you would just stop saying/doing/being things I don't like, we could all live happily ever after. The end.*

For me, the idea of embracing my choices as they relate to conflict—and I use the word *embrace* intentionally—altered my world.

Because here's the thing: The choice to love well sounds like a great idea. It sounds like unfolding freshly washed linens before anyone's had time to muddy them. But loving well—to listen, to speak with grace and truth, to address issues when we'd rather avoid issues, to be kind when we'd prefer to be cutting—isn't quite so easy when we've been hurt. Or misunderstood. Or feel dismissed, diminished, or displaced. Choices aren't simple in the middle of being mad. Or jealous. Or resentful. Or disappointed. Or accused.

But you already know this. You *live* this. I do too.

Except now, years after I first understood the significance of my choices in the midst of conflict, I'm more convinced than ever that choices matter—even, or maybe *especially*, when other people don't make good ones.

The choices we make in our most challenging moments are the choices that lead us to places of either greater connection or greater disconnection. Of increased harmony or increased hurt. Of more understanding and unity, or more misunderstanding and mayhem. Of real peace or real pain.

The truth is so simple it's often overlooked: in the midst of real-life conflict, our choices can change our relationships forever.

Is this always easy to embrace? I'd be lying if I said it was. But choosing to change my way of handling conflict to better align with God's game plan for handling conflict brings peace. It brings freedom. And, ultimately, it brings blessing.

Real-life conflict doesn't get resolved when other people choose to change.

It starts when I do.

Lord, thank You for loving me—the good parts and the ugly parts I'm sometimes tempted to hide. I confess what You already know: I need Your help for my relationships. I'm tired of handling conflict in ways I later regret. Forgive me for choices I've made that have caused hurt rather than healing. Fill my heart with hope in the possibility of learning new, better, and healthier ways of relating and resolving conflict. And, God, help me change myself when I'd really rather change someone else, amen.

PUTTING PEACE INTO PRACTICE

1. Do you have your own "some days I want to burn down the church" story—one where conflict made you think, feel, or do things you knew you'd later regret? If so, how did you process the conflict?

2. When I wrote "I am not responsible for how someone else handles conflict. I am only responsible for how I handle conflict," how does this truth convict you? In what way does it empower, inspire, or encourage you?

3. In the midst of conflict, do you tend to focus more on how the other person should change or on how you can change? Why do you think this is so?

4. How might making wise choices in the midst of conflict bring you more peace? How could it make you and your relationships healthier and holier? How might handling conflict God's way versus your way make the gospel evident?

TWO

WHY SO MUCH CONFLICT?

For every relational decision she made right, I could count two she made wrong. The only problem was she didn't know it. Her current conflict—the one she'd been telling me about—played on repeat, but it really didn't have to. There was a path to the peace she said she longed for.

I looked across the table into the warm brown eyes of this otherwise successful woman and silently weighed the pros and cons. Should I say something or not? She'd asked for my help, but I knew I held her tender heart in my hands. I also knew my silence would ultimately hurt her more. Sooner or later her poor choices would catch up with her, and she'd be left with the overwhelming burden of reversing relational devastation I knew she could've avoided in the first place.

Isn't that what we're all looking for—the know-how to steer clear of relational headaches before they happen? Or to at least repair them before they create total chaos in our lives?

I took a deep breath and decided to be honest and helpful, hoping she'd receive it well. She did. We chatted freely, sipping our lattes until the warm fall day became a chilly evening. As we gathered our things to go, she stopped midsentence, suddenly looking a little sheepish.

"I finally figured out what the real problem is."

I could hardly wait to hear what she'd say next.

"I don't know what I don't know."

I don't know what I don't know.

I could tell her admission made her feel exposed.

But where she felt broken, I saw bravery.

Where she felt fragile, I saw freedom.

Where she felt vulnerable, I saw victory.

We live in a world that tells us we must have it all together. All. The. Time. The secret we all know deep in our hearts—the secret only brave, honest, authentic women will reveal—is that we don't always have it all together. Truth be told, we *rarely* have it all together!

This side of heaven, conflict is part of life. However, conflict is largely misunderstood. Conflict isn't bad or good; conflict is neutral. The reality of conflict simply means we live among people who don't always think the way we think, prefer what we prefer, or do things the way we do things.

What makes conflict good or bad is not its presence but our practices in the midst of its presence.

The reason so many people feel like conflict is bad is because most of us haven't learned to deal with conflict in a way that makes it turn out good.

Sadly, many of our past experiences have taught us conflict doesn't make people feel closer, it makes people feel closed off. However, when handled according to God's blueprint, conflict can actually create *more* intimacy and *more* closeness between people. Consider these outcomes: an issue that once stood between two people is removed; a truth that once went unaddressed is discussed; a wound that once caused resentment is forgiven; an annoyance that once caused frustration is fixed.

So how exactly do we get God's blueprint and start making our negative experiences produce positive results? The first step is to take an honest look at how things *are* in comparison to how God *intended them to be*.

CAN'T WE JUST START OVER?

If you've ever been in a friendship or relationship that started off with sunshine and rainbows but ended with thunderclouds and lightning bolts, you've probably wished you could go back to the beginning and start over.

Which raises the question: How did *any* of us end up in relationships that are filled with conflict? After all, the human race didn't start this way. In the beginning there were no arguments. No disagreements. No drama. No division.

Actually, in the beginning, there were no problems at all. None. Nada. Zilch. Since many of us have lived with drama, conflict, and chaos our entire lives, it may be hard to even conceptualize what a conflict-free life would look like. It's worth a peek, if only to see what God originally intended for His children.

A quick exploration of the Genesis account unearths a world in which no opportunity for conflict existed because there were no unmet needs (and no sin, at least not yet). Think of this as a sort of "behind closed doors" look into how healthy, conflict-free relationships function, and a demonstration of why conflict happens if these human needs aren't met.

But here's where I want you to really pay attention: as we explore the needs the original couple met for one another, and as we observe what happens if these needs aren't fulfilled, you'll likely discover some "whys" behind some of your own most confusing conflicts.

THE ORIGINAL FAMILY LIVED CONNECTED

The human soul's deepest need is for connection. As Genesis 2:18 tells us, "The LORD God said, 'It is not good for the man to be alone.'" In 2020 our world was forever changed by a pandemic—one that left us physically isolated from one another. The profound problem of physical isolation is that it eventually leads to emotional and relational isolation. This. Is. Not. Good. God told us so from the beginning, but it's taken a worldwide crisis for many of us to see this for ourselves.

Physical connection with other people is not optional. And while we may endure necessary seasons of disengagement, human beings require the physical presence of others for emotional health.

Other people are to our spirits what oxygen is to our bodies.

It's possible to live under the same roof, reside in the same neighborhood, or work for the same company as others while also living isolated and separated from those same people. Often physical separation happens subtly: a new baby means I no longer see coworkers; my spouse's snoring means I sleep in a different bed; a move to a new city means I don't have a church home; our family's cell phones mean we look more at screens than at each other. Over time, we physically drift away from one another, then wonder why we feel empty, disconnected, and dissatisfied.

Here's where this becomes practical: disconnection is a breeding ground for conflict.

Empty, dissatisfied people can be easily agitated, overly argumentative, or a combination of both. Frankly, they spend too much time in their own brains, focused on their own perspectives and concerned about their own needs.

Additionally, it's easier to develop a false narrative around phantoms you rarely engage with than people you regularly see and talk to. Social scientists even have a name for our propensity to demonize those with whom we don't engage: *depersonalization*. How much easier is it to be cruel to someone we're convinced is a nonperson? Perhaps this is why cyberbullying runs rampant and the vitriol in our culture has reached epic proportions.

THEY VALUED AND APPRECIATED EACH OTHER

Physical connection with other people is merely the starting point. When God brought Eve to Adam, Adam was already aware of his personal void. God had taken him through an exercise of naming the animals, "but for Adam no suitable helper was found" (Genesis 2:20). So "the LORD God made a woman . . . and he brought her to the man" (Genesis 2:22). Who made Eve? God did! Eve had value because she was God's very own creation, made in His image.

What was true for Adam and Eve is true for us. Every human being is created by God and made in His image. Therefore, every person with whom we have a relationship has value. And so do *you*.

The original Hebrew renders Adam's first encounter with Eve something like this: "Whoa! Wow! This is now bone of my bone and flesh of my flesh!" (Genesis 2:23, my paraphrase). In other words,

Adam was thrilled to meet Eve because he appreciated the value Eve brought to his life.

And he said so.

In our relationships, unexpressed appreciation has the same effect as unappreciation; it's a conflict just waiting to happen.

When our kids were young, I often felt overworked and overlooked, as most moms of "littles" do. One day my husband came home and found me in tears, which is significant because I'm not a crier. (Except for in church—worship always makes me cry. But I digress.) I was sitting at the bottom of our stairs with my head in my hands and tears on my cheeks.

"What's wrong?" JP asked.

"No one appreciates me!" I wailed before launching into a ten-minute tirade of all the ways I served our family. JP remained silent. I finished the rant and resigned myself to accepting the fact that it would be many years before I felt appreciated.

But the next evening, JP surprised me. He'd generated a Certificate of Appreciation on his computer and had it framed! To this day, it remains one of my most treasured gifts, not only because my husband took the time to express his appreciation, but also because when I revealed how unappreciated I felt, he didn't counter with "Oh, yeah? *You* don't feel appreciated? What about *me*?"

He could have.

But he didn't.

A recent study found that the biggest indicator of workplace engagement was not how much money employees made but rather how recognized and appreciated employees felt.[1] The need to be appreciated can't be underestimated for relational health and peace in any environment.

No one starts a conflict when they feel appreciated and valued.

THEY LIVED NOTICED AND WANTED

Adam's response to Eve's arrival made it clear she was valued and appreciated, but Adam's response also shows us she was noticed and wanted. Who wouldn't want to be greeted with "Wow! You're here! Yippee!"? Sadly, the art of making others feel noticed and wanted is a skill sorely lacking in our society.

The need to be seen is woven into our DNA. Need proof? Think about small children who freely say things like "Look at me, Daddy!" "Watch me sing/dance/do a magic trick, Mommy!" Teenagers and adults take an estimated thirty-four billion selfies a year.[2] That, friends, is ninety-three million cries to be seen *every single day.*

Why the desperate need to be noticed? Because if you don't see me, I'm invisible, and if I'm invisible, I don't matter.

We *need* to matter.

In Dr. John Gottman's groundbreaking study conducted at the University of Washington, researchers found they could predict the success or failure of a relationship by observing a couple, not for years or months but in just one weekend. Although the study focused on marriage, the same predictors could apply to all relationships: family, friends, coworkers, and fellow Christians.

Interestingly, Dr. Gottman's findings corroborate the picture that provides the markers for healthy relationships painted in Genesis 2. The single determinant of whether a couple would stay together or divorce was not the absence of conflict. It wasn't common interests. It wasn't even shared values.

The single biggest indicator of relational success was the answer to this question: Do they pay attention to each other?

Dr. Gottman wrote, "The topic of conversation hardly mattered in these couples' willingness to connect. Some seemed determined to ignore their spouses, no matter how riveting or mundane the subject at hand. For example, we watched one wife completely ignore her husband as he tried to tell her about the harrowing military coup he had witnessed in Spain. In contrast, another couple seemed utterly entranced by one another's descriptions of how their mothers made bread."[3]

I believe the answer to this question—do they pay positive attention to each other?—can predict the success or failure of any relationship: parent and child, friend and friend, neighbor and neighbor. This is why technology has dealt a death blow to our relationships.

We've stopped noticing.

> CONFLICT IS THE UNNOTICED PERSON'S WAY OF SAYING, "PLEASE, SEE ME."

People who aren't noticed and don't feel wanted will do anything to be noticed—including instigate conflict. The child who feels overlooked may provoke a fight with his sibling. The spouse who feels neglected might be cranky or critical.

Conflict is the unnoticed person's way of saying, "Please, see me."

THEY BELONGED AND THEY BONDED

Not long ago, I was headed into my favorite coffee shop when I noticed two little girls walking in front of me hand in hand. As they walked, steps in sync, they swung their tightly clasped hands back and forth, back and forth. There was a freedom and intimacy in the way these girls related. It was clear they had an uncomplicated bond older girls and women don't often share.

Soon another little girl approached them, tentatively. My heart skipped a beat. Part of me wanted to call out to the two friends, "Please, be nice!" But I was merely an onlooker, so I remained silent. All I could do was hope.

The girls smiled. One of the two reached out her hand to the third, and as effortlessly as breathing, they allowed her to break into their circle of friendship. No one rolled her eyes. No one protested, "But I just want it to be us." No one questioned the decision.

She was there, so she was in.

When does it happen? I wondered. *At what moment do we stop holding out our hands and, in doing so, stop holding out our hearts? When do we stop enlarging our circle of relationships and start tightening it? At what point do we stop giving ourselves away and start guarding the way we give?*

The way the little girls at the coffee shop interacted with one another was pure. Accepting. Genuine. Their way is the way God intended relationships to be. Of this, I am certain.

In the same way, when God brought Eve to Adam, Adam reached out his hand, extended his heart, and welcomed her into the orbit of his life. Notice how he emphasized the similarities between himself and Eve: "Bone of my bones and flesh of my flesh" (Genesis 2:23). People bond based on commonality, not differences.

Does this mean we can only bond with those who are like us? Not at all! It simply means that to forge a connection we must first be willing to connect and then find something in common.

A mom who loves music and her child who likes football may not share the same interests, but they may share the same quirky sense of humor. Coworkers may not vote for the same candidate, but their professional goals are likely the same. Neighbors might be in different life stages, but they live in the same community.

Much of the disunity that divides our culture today can be directly linked to the current propensity to emphasize differences rather than similarities.

Each of us is unique, of course, but finding common ground

enables us to extend our hands and create bonds of belonging so our differences don't become dividers.

THEY HAD BOUNDARIES

As Adam and Eve's story unfolds, we see the need for appropriate boundaries: "That is why a man leaves his father and mother" (Genesis 2:24). From the very beginning, God built us for boundaries: "You are free to eat from any tree in the garden; *but you must not* eat from the tree of the knowledge of good and evil" (Genesis 2:16–17, emphasis added). In their bestselling book *Boundaries*, Dr. Henry Cloud and Dr. John Townsend wrote, "Boundaries help us keep the good in and the bad out."[4]

> AT THEIR CORE, HEALTHY BOUNDARIES KEEP US SAFE FROM TOXIC BEHAVIORS AND TOXIC PEOPLE WHO PERPETUATE CONFLICT.

At their core, healthy boundaries keep us safe from toxic behaviors and toxic people who perpetuate conflict.

But boundaries also help us keep our expectations realistic—expectations we place on ourselves as well as others. People without boundaries make themselves susceptible to hurt because they are often easy to take advantage of and frequently expect more than others can give.

Without boundaries, conflict is bound to happen.

THEY FELT ACCEPTED AND EXPERIENCED INTIMACY

One of the first emotions recorded in the Bible is found in Genesis 2:25: "Adam and his wife were both naked, and they *felt no shame*" (emphasis added). Exposed, vulnerable, and naked—emotionally and spiritually, as well as physically—they felt safe and free in one another's presence.

We have the same need for acceptance and intimacy in our closest relationships. I'm talking real, honest-to-goodness, authentic human intimacy with people who are safe.

How does this relate to conflict? Acceptance is the antidote for arguments.

Think about it: If you know I accept *you*, I can disagree with your opinion or choices without making you feel threatened. But in the absence of acceptance, a rejection of your opinion is perceived as a rejection of you. Conflict is virtually guaranteed.

There is more at play here, of course, and we'll explore this complicated issue in future chapters. But for now, it's important to note that without acceptance, conflicts are unlikely to be resolved and relationships are likely to dissolve.

DO YOU WANT WHAT GOD INTENDED?

So, there you have it. We've thrown back the curtains, opened up the doors, and peeked at the inner workings of the only two people in existence who experienced relational perfection and the complete absence of conflict.

No one in the garden of Eden ever fantasized about burning it down.

God has given us a glimpse of His original intention: a world where spiritual, emotional, and physical needs are met in relationship with our Creator and our relationships with one another.

You may be thinking, *Yeah, but that's not real life right now. My life is no garden of Eden.*

And you'd be right. Life isn't a garden of Eden. Needs go unmet. People have conflicts. Sin is real. This is our reality. But it's equally true that God has given us a blueprint for how to live now in the midst of our sin-laden, conflict-filled world.

No, we can't go back to the beginning, but we can move forward into new beginnings—a place where hope and healing reside. Wanna come?

Lord, help me recognize how unmet needs might be contributing to my relational conflict—both my unmet needs and others' unmet needs. When I spot areas of lack, empower me to fill the gap with Your wisdom, grace, and love. You long for Your children to live in harmony with You and each other. Help me be an agent of peace to fulfill Your plan, amen.

PUTTING PEACE INTO PRACTICE

When we explored the needs the original couple met for one another and what happens when these needs aren't fulfilled, you likely discovered some "whys" behind some of your own most confusing current conflicts.

1. Consider one relationship where you have conflict. Using a scale from 1 to 10 (1 being "not at all," and 10 being "almost always"), evaluate the level each need is met for both people:

   • Connected
   • Valued
   • Appreciated

- Noticed
- Wanted
- Sense of belonging
- Bonded
- Boundaries communicated and respected
- Accepted
- Intimacy

2. Circle the need that is least met. Are there any ways a lack in this area has contributed to your relational conflict?
3. What are a few tangible ways you can begin to meet this need? (Note: You may feel like *you* have a lack and wish someone would meet *your* need. However, remember that we can't change others; we can only change ourselves. Often as we change and grow, other people do too. Even if other people stay the same, we become different—more like Jesus.)

THREE

BUT FIRST, REMOVE THE LOG

I take a deep breath and open the door. The other patients look at me with suspicion. They've clearly got twenty-five—maybe thirty—years on me. I take my seat and try to look relaxed.

The gray-haired woman next to me leans over and whispers, "Honey, I think you're in the wrong place. This eye doctor checks for cataracts."

"Thank you, no, I'm in the right spot." Privately, I wonder if maybe she's right; perhaps I am in the wrong place.

After a few minutes, the nurse calls my name and takes me to a private room for examination. This feels insane. My sight is fine. I see fine. Everything's fine.

The doctor enters, shakes my hand, and asks if I know what cataracts are, exactly. I don't. Why should I? None of my friends has dealt with this before. He explains that a cataract is a cloudy area that forms in the lens of the eye, impairing vision. After his careful explanation I'm more certain than ever I don't have cataracts. He puts on his oversized examination goggles and begins his evaluation anyway. I can't help but think he looks like a giant fly.

"Wow. You definitely have a cataract in your right eye. And my goodness—how unusual for someone your age—you have a cataract in your left eye too."

"But I see fine."

He chuckles. "Well, you have cataracts, so I guess you don't."

"I promise, I see absolutely clearly."

"I don't think so."

"But my vision is normal."

He slides his little black stool with the roller wheels backward, takes off the oversized goggles, and looks me square in the eyes. I know he's not playing around now.

"Let me say this one last time, slowly. You. Have. Cataracts. Just because something seems normal does not mean it's healthy."

"Oh."

NORMAL DOES NOT (ALWAYS) MEAN HEALTHY

A couple of years ago I wrote a Bible study series that tackled the topics of healthy contentment, confidence, friendships, and family—all from a biblical vantage point. As part of my research, I spent an entire year studying, reading, observing, and asking women about their relationships. In the process, I discovered something unexpected: the single biggest difference between women who have healthy relationships and those who don't is not an absence of conflict but rather an accurate perspective about conflict. Healthy women see conflict, communication, and the possibility of connection differently than unhealthy women.

As it turns out, how we *view* things is as important as how we *do* things, because how we view things determines how we do things. Our perspective dictates our practices. Always.

No doubt, this is why Jesus gave us the following instructions:

"Judge not, that you be not judged. For with the judgment you pronounce you will be judged, and with the measure you use it will be measured to you. Why do you see the speck that is in your brother's eye, but do not notice the log that is in your eye? Or how can you say to your brother, 'Let me take the speck out of your eye,' when there is the log in your own eye? You hypocrite, first take the log out of your own eye, and then you will see clearly to take the speck out of your brother's eye." (Matthew 7:1–5 ESV)

Too many of us live like me in the eye doctor's office. We think we see our relationship issues clearly when, in fact, we don't. Our personal areas of unhealth have become so woven into the fabric of how we relate we have no idea our blind spots are, well . . . blind spots.

> HOW WE *VIEW* THINGS IS AS IMPORTANT AS HOW WE *DO* THINGS.

For starters, we're comfortable with our particular patterns of conflict management; they feel familiar, even if they're not always effective. We're settled in our communication habits. The way we see things, say things, and do things has become so ingrained in our way of relating we simply don't think about it. It's just the way things are. It's just the way *we* are.

From our vantage point, our conflicts, our communication, and our connection (or lack of it) are all so . . . normal. As a result, we focus on the shortcomings of others—the specks in their eyes—and skip right over our own contributions to our relational messes—the logs in ours. We don't examine ourselves long enough to see that a plank or log is there.

I find it interesting (and honestly, more than a little convicting) that Jesus launches His teaching with the command "Do not judge others." When our perspective collides with another's perspective, the great temptation is to look *first* at what the other person did wrong. We focus on what *they* said. How *they* acted. What *their* facial expression, tone of voice, and attitude conveyed. And in doing so, we judge others without first considering how we may have contributed to the conflict, even unintentionally.

Were we brash? Touchy? Uncaring? Unclear? Manipulative? Insecure? Passive? Dismissive? Critical? Controlling? Aloof? Absent? Avoidant? Did our own unhealthy way of relating obscure our ability to see the conflict and/or the other person accurately? Jesus warns us against assessing a relationship problem before first looking at ourselves. Frankly, in our broken humanness, it's all too easy (dare I say "normal"?) to focus on someone else's proverbial speck and miss our protruding log.

But, as my eye doctor aptly pointed out, normal doesn't always mean healthy. Sometimes someone must show us it's not.

Remember, *how we view things determines how we do things*, especially in our relationships. Perhaps this is why Satan was so determined to get Eve to see things from his vantage point.

IF THE GARDEN DIDN'T BURN DOWN, HOW COME WE DON'T LIVE THERE ANYMORE?

In the previous chapter we discussed how the original couple lived conflict-free. Obviously, no two people since Adam and Eve have lived in a conflict-free world. So what happened? Read the account written below, paying special attention to the words *eyes* and *see*.

> Now the serpent was more crafty than any of the wild animals the LORD God had made. He said to the woman, "Did God really say, 'You must not eat from any tree in the garden'?" The woman said to the serpent, "We may eat fruit from the trees in the garden, but God did say, 'You must not eat fruit from the tree that is in the middle of the garden, and you must not touch it, or you will die.'" "You will not certainly die," the serpent said to the woman. "For God knows that when you eat from it your eyes will be opened, and you will be like God, knowing good and evil." When the woman saw that the fruit of the tree was good for food and pleasing to the eye, and also desirable for gaining wisdom, she took some and ate it. She also gave some to her husband, who was with her, and he ate it. Then the eyes of both of them were opened, and they realized they were naked; so they sewed fig leaves together and made coverings for themselves. (Genesis 3:1–7)

Did you catch the beginning of Eve's downfall? Satan's promise, "your eyes will be opened," and her response, "when [she] saw"? Satan knew that how Eve viewed the fruit would determine what she would do with the fruit. He got her eyes off God and His goodness and turned them onto herself and the fruit.

If we could have stood shoulder to shoulder with Eve, knowing how her faulty perception would lead to a fatal choice and affect all relationships, for all people and for all time, we'd certainly have jerked the fruit from her hand. We'd have protested, "Don't do it, girl! Don't do it!"

Why did Eve make the choice she made? Why do *any* of us make the choices we make?

Quite simply: perspective. Our perspective influences our practices. Our attitudes affect our actions.

How we view things *always* determines how we do things.

What does this mean for you and me and how we handle disagreements, division, and dissension?

We must see God accurately, we must see ourselves accurately, we must see others accurately, and we must see the issue accurately. A breakdown in any one of these areas will mean a breakdown in how effectively we handle conflict.

Conflict cannot be resolved in a healthy way if we see God as indifferent to our conflicts. He's not. God cares *deeply* about how His children relate to one another. Scripture is filled with instructions for how we are to respond in the midst of our real-life conflict struggles.

In addition, conflict cannot be resolved in a healthy way if we fail to see others as they are. Countless conflicts come from faulty perceptions, like "I thought you didn't care because you didn't say anything," "I just assumed you'd know I wanted help," "When you didn't call, I figured you were mad," or "I didn't feel like I could say what I really thought." If the way we see others is inaccurate, our assessment of the circumstances surrounding the conflict will be inaccurate too.

Further, when our perception is off, conflict—and the resulting hurt, anger, or frustration it generates—can cause us to see others as objects, obstacles, or the opposition.

What does this mean in real life?

If I see you as an **object**:	You're a stereotype, so I dehumanize you.
If I see you as an **obstacle**:	You're an impediment, so I need to remove you, your behavior, or your opinion.
If I see you as the **opposition**:	You're the enemy, so I demonize you and can't listen to you.

I'm guessing you can pinpoint situations you've experienced personally, observed on social media, or watched on the news where one or more of these scenarios played out. If so, you know seeing other people as objects, obstacles, or the opposition never resolves conflict or restores peace.

Finally, if we want real hope for relationship restoration, we must also see ourselves, and our role in the conflict, accurately. After weathering their own storm of infidelity, my friend, author and speaker Jill Savage, and her husband, Mark, now work with couples in crisis. Jill wrote:

> Mark has been reading a powerful book that he said described Mark 1.0—the one who thought leaving his marriage would take care of his problems ten years ago. At that time, he had no idea how much his personal struggle with rejection was fueling his wrong thinking about what the problem was in his life. He couldn't see clearly. We all struggle with our vision in some way. We have blind spots where we lack insight or an awareness of places we still need to grow. Our blindness keeps us pointing the finger at others instead of looking at ourselves. I (Jill) was blind to my lack of compassion before our marriage crisis. As we healed and went to counseling, I began to see how my lack of compassion was affecting my relationships negatively. This awareness gave me the opportunity to grow! I could see clearly![1]

FOUR COMMON MISCONCEPTIONS ABOUT CONFLICT

Since it's imperative that we see conflict accurately, let's examine four of the most common misconceptions surrounding conflict and compare them with what God says.

MISCONCEPTION #1

It's normal, and even okay, to handle my anger, frustration, hurt, and disappointment in whatever way feels right in the moment.

Truth: Since I'm a Christian, God has a new—better and healthier—way for me to handle my anger, frustration, hurt, and disappointment. I was created to be like God in true righteousness and holiness. That means I should seek to handle the hard stuff in a holy way. My goal in conflict is not to get my way but to glorify God. Degrading words, bitterness, rage, anger, slander, or malice—these actions should have no place in my life, not even when I'm mad. Instead, I should choose to be kind and compassionate, forgiving others because I am forgiven by God.

> You were taught, with regard to your former way of life, to put off your old self, which is being corrupted by its deceitful desires; to be made new in the attitude of your minds; and to put on the new self, created to be like God in true righteousness and holiness. . . .
>
> Do not let any unwholesome talk come out of your mouths, but only what is helpful for building others up according to their needs, that it may benefit those who listen. And do not grieve the Holy Spirit of God, with whom you were sealed for the day of redemption. Get rid of all bitterness, rage and anger, brawling and slander, along with every form of malice. Be kind and

compassionate to one another, forgiving each other, just as in Christ God forgave you. (Ephesians 4:22–24, 29–32)

MISCONCEPTION #2

Conflict pits me against another person—my spouse, my child, my sibling, my parent, my coworker, my in-laws.

Truth: Every person is my neighbor, and believers are all members of one body—Christ's. We are on the same team, even if it doesn't seem like it sometimes. My real enemy is not another person but hell itself. When it *feels* like another person is my adversary, I need to remember they are not. God has designed relationships to function best when I choose to behave based on truth rather than feelings or perception.

> Therefore each of you must put off falsehood and speak truthfully to your neighbor, for we are all members of one body. (Ephesians 4:25)

> For our struggle is not against flesh and blood, but against the rulers, against the authorities, against the powers of this dark world and against the spiritual forces of evil in the heavenly realms. (Ephesians 6:12)

MISCONCEPTION #3

Christians shouldn't get mad; anger is a sin.

Truth: Anger is an emotion. Emotions are not sin. However, what I do with my anger can easily become sin if I let it. *In* my anger—and God assumes we *will* experience anger—I must not use anger as an excuse to sin.

> "In your anger do not sin." (Ephesians 4:26)

MISCONCEPTION #4

Unresolved anger is no big deal.

Truth: God tells me to resolve disagreements quickly, otherwise the Enemy can unravel my relationships even further—sowing seeds like bitterness, resentment, or the desire for revenge, which can have deeper ramifications down the road.

> Do not let the sun go down while you are still angry, and do not give the devil a foothold. (Ephesians 4:26–27)

————o————

Why take the time to identify misconceptions about anger and conflict? Because my thoughts *about* conflict affect my actions *in* conflict.

- If I think conflict is bad, I'll avoid it at all costs. This is not healthy.
- If I think Christians aren't supposed to get angry, I won't speak the truth, and I'll be passive-aggressive instead. This is not healthy.
- If I think conflict means one person wins and one person loses, I'll gear up for a fight or avoid conflict altogether. This is not healthy.
- If I think it's okay to let my anger fester, I'll store up resentment and bitterness. This is not healthy.

Are you starting to see why the way we view conflict is so important?

Most of us develop our conflict styles and coping strategies in childhood, yet no one drags out a whiteboard, tells us to pull up a chair, and says, "Today I'm going to teach you how to handle conflict." Instead, we live with a mother who skirts around issues to keep the peace at all costs, or we live with a father who explodes at the slightest inconvenience. In the still, dark of our rooms at night, our little ears hear slammed doors or raised voices. We wake up to indirect manipulation rather than direct confrontation. We watch family members play victim rather than play fair, or we watch them walk away rather than work through things.

In short, experience becomes our teacher.

Because these experiences happen early in our development and occur over a long period of time, we can easily begin to believe these conflict strategies are normal—because, for us, they are.

But again, as I learned in my eye doctor's office, normal doesn't always mean healthy.

If we are blessed with godly role models, though, we see people talking things out, working things through, taking personal responsibility, and forgiving offenses. In short, we see people who marry wisdom with grace.

NORMAL DOESN'T ALWAYS MEAN HEALTHY.

This is why the starting point for handling conflict well must begin with our willingness to identify our "planks" or "logs," as Jesus instructed. Only then can we see clearly enough to help others too.

WHAT'S YOUR CONFLICT STYLE?

Part of how we can identify our logs is to understand our personal conflict styles. Generally, people fall into one of the following categories. Read the following list to identify your conflict style. Please note that most of these styles were first identified by the Thomas-Kilmann Conflict Mode Instrument.[2]

THE COMPETITOR

- Likes to argue and debate. Assertive. Believes in standing up for oneself and defending opinions. Can be threatening or intimidating. May place "being right" over the relationship.
- **Goal:** to win; to control an outcome or a person
- **Resulting feelings:** feels satisfied, powerful, or prideful upon "winning"; feels impotent or angry and will likely blame others upon "losing"

THE COMPROMISER

- Intimidated by direct confrontation. Seeks a quick middle-ground solution. Doesn't always fully understand or agree with the other's perspective, but gives in to end the conflict or preserve the relationship.
- **Goal:** a quick resolution with minimal conflict
- **Resulting feelings:** dissatisfaction, since parties generally focus on what they lost in the compromise

THE AVOIDER

- Pretends conflict never happened or doesn't exist. Excuses others' bad behaviors. Thinks, *If we don't bring it up, it will blow over.* Harbors feelings. Doesn't express views. Allows conflict to fester until it becomes too big to ignore.

- **Goal:** no conflict
- **Resulting feelings:** confusion over what went wrong since feelings aren't verbalized; internalized hurt, anger, or resentment

THE ACCOMMODATOR

- Gives in to others' preferences or views. Allows needs of the group to overwhelm their own, which may never be stated. Sees preserving the relationship as most important. Can make peace and move forward but can also harbor feelings of resentment toward the other party.
- **Goal:** keep peace
- **Resulting feelings:** powerless, voiceless, like a doormat

THE MANIPULATOR

- Fears expressing thoughts, feelings, and opinions directly, so expresses them through backdoor channels. Often uses other people to tell someone what they think, feel, or want. May also use the silent treatment, withdrawal, disapproval, guilt, shame, nagging, lying, or pouting. Is passive-aggressive.
- **Goal:** to control
- **Resulting feelings:** powerful if others acquiesce; fearful, hurt, or angry if others don't acquiesce

THE COLLABORATOR

- Seeks a win-win solution to conflict. Listens to understand others' viewpoints. Focuses on areas of agreement and goals.

Thinks creatively to resolve the problem without concessions.
Is both assertive and cooperative.

- **Goal:** a solution that satisfies everyone
- **Resulting feelings:** satisfaction, peace, harmony

So, having now read these descriptions, which one do you believe you are? Can you identify ways you handle conflict that might have been blind spots until now?

Unless your conflict style is the Collaborator, you have room to grow in the way you handle disagreements and disputes. Welcome to the human race.

The good news is if you find yourself thinking, *Well, I obviously have room to grow*—congratulations!—you already possess the single most important quality for handling conflicts well, the one thing no relationship can succeed without.

Want to know what it is? Keep reading.

Lord, today I choose to examine the log in my own eye. Remove any falsehood, any misconceptions, or any wrong way of relating that's become normal for me but isn't honoring to You. Although this is a little scary to ask, please open my eyes in the middle of my conflicts to show me ways I might be contributing to the problem. Thank You for having good intentions for me—a plan and a purpose to conform me to be more like You and to experience more peace, amen.

PUTTING PEACE INTO PRACTICE

Let's revisit four common misconceptions about conflict:

- It's normal, and even okay, to handle my anger, frustration, hurt, and disappointment in whatever way feels right in the moment.
- Conflict pits me against another person—my spouse, my child, my sibling, my parent, my coworker, my in-laws.
- Christians shouldn't get mad; anger is a sin.
- Unresolved anger is no big deal.

1. Which of these misconceptions have you believed? How has your misconception hindered your ability to resolve conflict well?
2. One of the most important aspects of resolving conflict in a healthy, holy way is seeing accurately. As a mental exercise, consider a recent conflict. Did you see

   - God accurately,
   - the issue accurately,
   - yourself accurately, and
   - the other person accurately?

   What do you think God wants you to learn about how you see things moving forward?
3. When we don't see other people accurately, we see them as objects, obstacles, or opposition. As you reconsider a recent conflict, can you identify any way you've seen the

other person as one of these three? How do you think God wants you to see the person?

4. What unhealthy ways of handling conflict did you witness in your childhood? What healthy ways of handling conflict did you experience?

5. Review the conflict styles listed at the end of the chapter. Which conflict style best represents you? How would you like to grow in the way you handle conflict?

FOUR

THE ONE QUALITY NO RELATIONSHIP CAN SURVIVE WITHOUT

"What do you think it takes to have a good relationship?"

JP finished tying his shoe, stood up, and answered my question. "It's not what I used to think."

"What do you mean?" I'd been curious about what he thought before, but now I was positively intrigued.

"I used to believe a good relationship is a result of open communication, shared values, mutual respect, and love. You know, the stuff you read about in every relationship book. But as vital as those things are, they aren't the most important thing. There's something else—a quality that, if missing, makes all these good things eventually crumble. This is true not just for a marriage relationship but for all relationships."

Crumble? Seriously? Was JP right? What one, single quality is absolutely necessary for any relationship to thrive? For every conflict to be resolved?

Fast-forward twenty-five years. Our son stood at the altar with his bride. Broad, beaming smiles on both their faces told everyone in attendance this was a day they'd always remember. After a prayer and a blessing, they turned toward one another to recite their personalized wedding vows. Our son spoke first; one line in particular caught my attention.

"I promise to seek to understand more than I seek to be understood."

I'm not sure our son knew it then, but this attitude is the essence of what his dad told me decades earlier on the fateful morning we talked about relationship survival. If kept, the promise my son made on his wedding day will be a game changer and a relationship saver. After a wedding comes a marriage. After the birth of a child comes parenting. After the acceptance of a job comes work. After the introduction comes friendship. What do all these circumstances have in common? Up close and personal human contact. Day in, day out.

Human contact inevitably leads to human conflict. This isn't a bad thing; it's simply a real thing.

But as our contacts become closer (tighter inner circles) and our connections become broader (wider outer circles), the potential for conflict multiplies.

This means in real life—the lives you and I actually live—a conflict with a child will crop up just as a conflict with a coworker gets resolved. No sooner does a marital issue get squared away than a mother-in-law issue surfaces. The never-ending potential for conflict can leave us overwhelmed unless we know two things: (1) the root of all human conflict is the desire to control, and (2) the most important ingredient to a healthy relationship is an attitude that must permeate our heart, mind, and soul.

That attitude is humility.

Human contact means human conflict. But the good news is

two humble people can work through just about any conflict life can dish out. However, serve up a plate of conflict to two prideful people, and the result is about as predictable as letting a three-year-old order dinner. You might like what you get, but probably not.

So, if humility is the single quality no relationship can survive without, it's vital to understand what humility is and what humility isn't.

WHAT IS HUMILITY?

Humility is one of the most misunderstood and overlooked attributes necessary for conflict resolution. Let's face it: Humility's not sexy like emotional chemistry. It's not practical like empathetic listening. It's not even a no-brainer like decent communication skills. Without humility we can easily become manipulative, calculating, controlling, or uncaring. And without humility, other people won't (genuinely) cooperate with our efforts to resolve conflict.

Humility is the superpower necessary for healthy human relationships.

Humility enables us to see problems from another's perspective, to apologize when wrong, to forgive when wronged, to examine how we might have contributed to a conflict, to learn from mistakes, to follow God's instructions as we relate to others, and to trust God with outcomes. Humility is not a mark of weakness but a mark of strength. Biblical humility doesn't make us doormats for exploitation but doorways for conversation.

BIBLICAL HUMILITY DOESN'T MAKE US DOORMATS FOR EXPLOITATION BUT DOORWAYS FOR CONVERSATION.

CONFLICT WITH HUMILITY	CONFLICT WITHOUT HUMILITY
Seeks to understand and be understood	Seeks only to be understood
Values the relationship	Values being right
Sees one's own contribution to the conflict	Sees only another's contribution to the conflict
Speaks truth	Avoids speaking truth
Speaks factually	Forms judgments; uses hyperbole or name-calling
Is concerned	Is controlling
Speaks respectfully	Speaks rudely
Discusses the issue	Demeans the person
Apologizes when wrong	Sees no need to apologize
Owns one's behavior	Blames behavior on others or circumstances
Sees how conflict affects all	Sees how conflict affects self
Is authentic and sincere	Is manipulative, pouty, or passive-aggressive
Is helpful	Is hurtful
Is sensitive to others	Is insensitive to others
Has a win-win attitude	Has a win-lose attitude
Works through	Walks away
Learns from past mistakes	Refuses to learn and repeats past mistakes
Listens more than talks	Talks more than listens
Thinks: *What do I want in the long term?*	Thinks: *What do I want right now?*
Is honest	Is dishonest

Does what is right in God's eyes	Does what is right in own eyes
Prays up	Powers up

In Scripture, the word translated as *humility* is defined as "an inside-out virtue produced by comparing ourselves *to the Lord* (rather than to others)." For us as Christians, this means "living *in complete dependence on the Lord*, i.e. with no reliance on *self* (the flesh)."[1]

Humility isn't merely a handy tool but a hallmark of the believer's life. God specifically instructs us to be humble in the way we relate to others. Ephesians 4:2 says, "Be completely humble and gentle; be patient, bearing with one another in love." In 1 Peter 3:8–9 we're told, "Finally, all of you, be like-minded, be sympathetic, love one another, be compassionate and humble. Do not repay evil with evil or insult with insult. On the contrary, repay evil with blessing, because to this you were called so that you may inherit a blessing."

Of course, all this sounds appealing—doable, even—when our spouse is kind, our coworker is congenial, our friend is caring, and our fellow Christian is compassionate. But let any one of these folks treat us in a way we perceive as unkind, uncaring, or uncompassionate, and humility won't typically be the trait that gets triggered. Far from it. We might even think, *Humility? There's no way! Sorry, but I'm not about to let myself get walked all over.*

Perhaps this is our gut reaction because we equate humility with weakness rather than strength. When we tether the choice to be humble with humiliation, we've fundamentally misunderstood humility. Humility is "strength restrained." When Spirit-produced inner strength locks arms with Spirit-produced self-control— which is essentially what happens when we choose to be humble—we acquire the wisdom to know when to speak up, when to stand up, and when to shut up.

This restrained strength gives us eyes to see beneath surface issues, to the deeper issues that drive surface conflict. With this expanded vision, we know the best way to respond.

Contrary to popular opinion, humility is not timidity or insecurity. Humble people speak their minds, share their viewpoints, express their needs, and vocalize dissatisfaction. Heck, humble people even get angry! But the *way* they speak, share, and express themselves takes other people into account. A humble person views conflict through the lens of me *and* you, rather than me *versus* you.

During our first year of marriage, JP and I were in the middle of a conflict. I wanted him to see my perspective, and he wanted me to see his perspective. Both of us were so intent on getting our points across, though, that neither of us listened to the other. Emotions flared. Words flew. Voices were raised. Then, almost out of nowhere, JP uttered one sentence that completely defused the argument.

"Donna, I'm on your team."

Immediately, the anger that had been thick just moments before dissipated. Tensions melted, my muscles relaxed, and my brain moved from fight-or-flight mode to a more rational "we can figure this out" mode. Those four words—*I'm on your team*—moved us from "me against you" to "me and you against the problem."

This is the power of humility; it enables us to handle conflict in a way that helps rather than hurts. Again, humility makes us doorways, not doormats.

Consider Jennifer, a mom, and her teenage daughter, Olivia. Generally, Olivia's a good kid with a sweet disposition, but today she's been sassy and sulky. In truth, Olivia's behavior hasn't just frustrated Jennifer; it's hurt her feelings. Jennifer thinks, *If she rolls her eyes at me again or makes one more snarky remark, I'm going to let her have it!* Cue the yelling and door slamming.

If Jennifer puts on a heart of humility, she might dig deeper into the source of Olivia's behavior. She already knows "sassy and sulky" isn't Olivia's typical style, so she asks Olivia what's going on. Jennifer discovers Olivia's acting out because a friend snubbed her. Knowing this, Jennifer might decide to correct Olivia's behavior while also acknowledging her feelings, saying something like "I'm so sorry you weren't invited. I know that hurts, and I understand why you're upset. But Olivia, I love you and am here for you. It's not okay for you to take your anger and hurt out on me."

If Jennifer isn't humble, she'll likely respond out of habit or hurt. She may even respond in ways that will only make the conflict worse, such as "I don't care what you're going through. Snap out of it." "Your friend left you out? Well, I'm going to call her mom right now and give her a piece of my mind!" Or "What did you do to make her leave you out? I'll bet you did something." Any of these responses will only increase the drama, not relieve the drama.

In the first scenario, Olivia will likely feel cared for, even while being corrected. But in the second scenario, Olivia will likely feel controlled. Jennifer and Olivia's conflict will move from miserable to miserable on steroids.

Cared for or *controlled.* Remember these words. We'll come back to them in later chapters.

Or consider Beth. She loves her job but is crushed to learn one of her coworkers has been talking behind her back. Beth's first response is hurt. She thinks, *Why would she talk about me like that? I thought we were friends.* But the more Beth thinks about the malicious gossip her coworker spread, she's not just mad but furious: *Two can play this game, you backstabber.*

Of course, Beth doesn't say this out loud; Beth's a Christian. Christians don't say things like this (gasp!).

But they think them.

Then they react.

Often, they couch their response to conflict in sly digs, backhanded compliments, verbal assaults, passive-aggressive avoidance, or secret whispers—followed by something religious-sounding, such as "Bless her heart. We need to pray for her."

Left to our own devices, hurt people hurt people. When hurt people hurt people, the cycle of conflict-induced headaches and heartaches plays on repeat. You hurt me? Then I'll hurt you. The volume and intensity increase with every spin around the record.

Until someone decides to change the music and respond with humility. Because—and this is key—while hurt people hurt people, humble people lay the groundwork for healthy conflict resolution.

So how does humble Beth handle her coworker? It depends. Beth might try "speaking the truth in love" (Ephesians 4:15)—confronting her by saying something like "Hey, this is awkward, but I heard what you said about me in the break room. It's important to me to have respectful relationships with my coworkers, including you. I hope you feel the same. I wanted to come directly to you with this issue, rather than discuss it among the other staff and foster more office drama. In the future, if you have a problem with me professionally or personally, please talk to me rather than others first. I don't intend to discuss this with anyone else, and I hope you'll do the same so we can have the best work environment possible."

Or Beth might let the comment go, release her bitterness, and love her enemy.

Whatever Beth decides, she'll search the Scriptures to figure out how God wants her to respond. She won't make her choice out of fear and pretend peacekeeping is the same as peacemaking (since it's not). She won't make her choice out of fury, rationalizing her anger by saying, "She had it coming."

Beth will humble herself before God and decide to handle conflict His way. A humble person prays, *God, my feelings tell me to react one way, but Your Word tells me to react another way. Though it's hard, I choose Your way.* It's nearly impossible to be humble toward others if we aren't first humble toward God. Because—and let's be honest here—when we *need* to practice humility the most, we *want* to practice humility the least.

Humility happens when our faith trumps our feelings.

> WHEN WE *NEED* TO PRACTICE HUMILITY THE MOST, WE *WANT* TO PRACTICE HUMILITY THE LEAST.

HUMILITY AFFECTS THE STORIES WE TELL OURSELVES

The human brain is wired to make sense of our circumstances. We assign meaning and motives to answer the questions "Why did this happen?" and "What should I do?" Circumstances surrounding conflict are no exception.

In every conflict, we tell ourselves a story about the other person and about ourselves. For example: my coworker dominated the meeting because he doesn't value women; our friend didn't include us because she's upset over something we said; my spouse is quiet because he doesn't want to be with me. We concoct such narratives to explain behavior. Yet a humble (and wise!) person owns the fact that the motives she assigns to another's behavior may, or may not, be accurate.

Not surprisingly, the stories we weave during conflict almost always paint us in the best possible light and the other person in the worst possible light. We are the innocent victim; they are the guilty villain. Every time we think about the conflict, our brains mine for supporting evidence to back up our narrative. Before long, we're confident the way we see the situation is 100 percent right.

A humble person asks God (and sometimes others) for the wisdom to see conflict clearly, which means examining their own role in the conflict. A humble person has the strength of character to ask, "Did I contribute to this conflict in any way, even inadvertently? If so, how?" A humble person takes responsibility for their role in a conflict but doesn't take responsibility for the other person's role. Remember, a humble person is a doorway, not a doormat.

A humble person reins in the stories she concocts in her head, acknowledging that these narratives are always filtered through the lens of hurt, misunderstanding, or perceived wrongs. In fact, numerous studies show that the typical accuracy rate in assessing other people's motives is a mere 20 percent and only rises to 30 percent with people we know well.[2] This means 70–80 percent of the motives we assign to the other person's behavior is flat-out wrong!

If you're like me, you might be thinking, *I could see how that statistic might be true for most people, but I'm not most people. I know the motive.* (Just keepin' it real here.) I hope you can see the prideful irony in a thought like this. A humble person realizes the stories she tells herself before she has all the facts are, in fact, just stories—tales that may, or may not, turn out to be true.

DOES HUMILITY WORK?

I sat halfway back in the lecture hall in my interpersonal communications class at UCLA. The air hung heavy, and the room felt cramped. My classmates and I had jammed ourselves into whatever seat we could find to hear the world-renowned professor discuss conflict. Finally the tall, well-dressed blond woman we'd all come to hear took her place behind the podium.

"At its root, all conflict is really a power struggle," the professor explained.

Though I didn't want to miss a moment of the lecture, I mentally tuned out for a minute as my mind reeled through the various forms of conflict I'd experienced in my life. Were they all really power struggles and not actually about the issues I thought they were about?

When I tuned back in, I heard her say each conflict or power struggle answers these questions:

- Who gets their way?
- Who's in charge?
- Who is right?
- Who gets heard?
- Who's in control?
- Who gets their needs met?
- Who gets their feelings acknowledged?
- Who gets validated?
- Who gets their desire fulfilled?

Yep. This pretty much rang true for every interpersonal conflict I'd experienced.

If she was right about conflict being a power struggle, then that would explain why humility works. Humility is kryptonite to power and pride.

Maybe you remember the baseball bat game from when you were a kid—the game where you place your hand on the bottom of the bat, then another person puts their hand above yours. Back and forth—your hand, then their hand—until the person whose hand lands at the top of the bat wins. This is conflict. Your way? No, their way. Your perspective? No, their perspective. Your idea? No, their idea. Your feelings? No, their feelings. Back and forth, back and forth, until someone's way, perspective, idea, or feelings come out on top. Winner takes all.

Humility doesn't play this game. In real-life relationships, if one person wins and the other loses, ultimately no one wins. The winner gets "control" in the short run, but in the long run, the loser leaves the relationship, either actively or passively—which, ironically, is the loser's way of regaining control.

Years ago, I spoke on the topic of healthy relationships at a large Christian conference center and briefly touched on the importance of humility. After my message and all the other attendees had left the room, the director of the camp approached me.

"Did you notice my daughter during the session?" she asked.

I had. The director and her twentysomething daughter had been seated side by side on the front row during my message.

"That wouldn't have been possible one year ago."

"Tell me more." Intuitively, I knew the woman standing before me had battled for a good relationship with her daughter. And won.

The camp director took a deep breath and began. "My daughter was a delightful child, but when she hit the teen years, things changed. Every conversation, and practically every situation, became a conflict. I lived a nightmare. It broke my heart to see the way other mothers and daughters enjoyed being together while my daughter and I could hardly whisper a 'good morning' without a fight. I did everything I knew to do, and I prayed every way I knew how to pray, but all my efforts did nothing to change her behavior or our relationship. On the outside our family looked fine, but the truth was we lived in a war zone. My daughter moved out the minute she turned eighteen, and we barely spoke for two and a half years."

"What happened to change all that?" I wondered aloud.

"I became so desperate for some kind of connection with my daughter that I finally tried something I'd never tried before. I invited her to lunch, with this promise: 'You have the freedom to tell me everything I did that hurt you, angered you, or embarrassed you as you were growing up, and I will simply listen.'

"To my surprise, she agreed. Our drive to the restaurant was awkward. We barely spoke, except about safe topics like the weather. But once we arrived, found a table, and ordered our lunch, I re-iterated my promise: 'You talk, and I'll listen.'

"At first my daughter seemed tentative. She tiptoed into the conversation, told me one small thing that hurt her. Looking back, I realize she was testing the waters to see if I'd be true to my word. I nodded and kept my promise not to respond. Then she told me another thing she felt I had done wrong. Then another. Once she realized my promise was genuine and I was actually going to let her talk without interruption, a dam broke. All the hurt, anger, and resentment she'd spent years holding back spilled out faster than I could mentally process.

"I'd wanted nothing more than to be a godly, loving mother who enjoyed a loving relationship with my child, but there we sat— broken mother, broken daughter. All my failures laid bare.

"It was the hardest lunch of my life.

"Everything in me wanted to explain—'Don't you remember

what was going on at the time?'—or justify—'I made that decision because . . .'—or defend myself—'What I did was right'—or deflect—'Well, you were no picnic in the park to live with either.' Honestly, I didn't agree with about half of what she said. But that was never the point.

"So I sat in silence and kept my promise.

"I tried to remain upbeat on the drive home, but I felt emotionally pummeled. Weirdly, though, I noticed a lightness in my daughter that I hadn't seen in years. We hadn't driven far when she turned to me with a smile that reminded me of her as a little girl. 'Mom, that was the best conversation we've ever had,' she said.

"That was the day our relationship changed."

After the woman standing before me finished her story, I almost couldn't speak. I didn't want to muddy her beautiful tale of restoration and redemption with empty words. She'd experienced—no, she'd *lived*—something holy, born out of her choice to be humble. She had a daughter by her side to prove it.

Humility was the hardest option. It always is. That's why humility is born of strength, not weakness. Only the strongest among us can practice humility.

Pride says, "I control." Humility says, "I care."

Pride says, "I want you to know I'm right." Humility says, "I want you to know I value this relationship."

Pride says, "You or me." Humility says, "You *and* me."

JESUS, OUR EXAMPLE

The best model of humility, of course, was Jesus. Perfectly right, He allowed Himself to be wronged in order to extend relationship to broken, sinful people like you and me. His humility was the greatest demonstration of His strength.

Jesus said in Matthew 11:29, "Take my yoke upon you and learn from me, for I am gentle and humble in heart, and you will find rest for your souls."

Here, *humble* means God-reliant rather than self-reliant. The Son of God lived out His human relationships dependent on His relationship with the Father. If we're going to speak and act with humility, we'll need to live dependent on our relationship with God too. Frankly, our natural inclination *not* to be humble is too strong to overcome without God's help.

But notice the result of learning the way of Jesus: "You will find rest for your souls." In the original Greek (the language of the New Testament), *rest* means "inner tranquility." So, the verse could read, "Learn from Me, and you will find inner tranquility for your souls." What does this mean for us as we navigate the choppy waters of human conflict?

Humility calms down the inner chaos conflict churns up.

The path to peace in our relationships—with God and with others—and the path to peace in our souls is never paved with pride. It's paved with humility.

So, on that fateful day when I asked my husband, JP, what he thought it took to have a good relationship, what was his answer?

"Humility."

As it turns out, he was right.

God, help me be humble, first in my relationship with You and also in my relationships with others. I have to be honest, God: humility feels unfamiliar, especially when I just want all the conflict to stop, or when I've been hurt and feel wronged.

Help me to grasp what humility is and, just as important, what humility is not. Help me move from "me versus you" to "me and you" in the way I think, speak, and act. Show me how to respond according to Your Word, especially when I feel hurt, angry, or misunderstood. When I fail, grant me the humility to apologize and learn from my mistakes. Thank You for teaching me the one thing my relationships cannot survive without—humility, amen.

PUTTING PEACE INTO PRACTICE

1. Does the word *humility* have a negative connotation for you, or a positive one? Does the idea that "humility makes us doorways, not doormats" change your perspective on humility in any way? If so, how?

2. How does knowing that conflict is really a power struggle provide insight into a current conflict you're facing?

3. Look again at the list of ways we handle conflict without humility versus with humility. Which list best represents the way you currently handle conflict? Which list would you like to represent the way you handle conflict?

4. James 4:6 says, "God opposes the proud but gives grace to the humble" (ESV). How does this truth motivate you to choose humility over pride?

5. How can you approach a current conflict as "me and you" rather than "me versus you"? List some specific things you could say or do.

FIVE

WHY WE GET MAD
(AND WHAT TO DO ABOUT IT)

I reach down to grab the dish soap from underneath the sink. *Ugh! The door hinge is still broken. How many times have I asked my husband to fix it? Too many to count. I'll say something again tonight.*

JP comes home, but the evening is rushed. Dinner. Homework. Baths. Bed. It's late when I pull the cabinet door open for what seems like the hundredth time in a day. This time, though, it falls off. The heavy wood door bangs hard on the floor before landing on my foot. I want to scream. This should have been fixed *weeks* ago.

I march into the family room, where JP has just picked up the remote to settle in with a good movie. I don't care.

I. Don't. *Care.*

He needs to change, and if it causes a fight, so be it.

Sadly, this scene played out more than once in the early days of our marriage. If it wasn't about door hinges, it was about yard work. If it wasn't about yard work, it was about something else—but always the same pattern: I ask. He says he'll do it. He doesn't do it.

I ask again. He apologizes and says he'll get around to it. He means to, but he doesn't. I nag. He *still* doesn't do it. I throw a fit.

It gets done.

The last day this crazy cycle of conflict played itself out was sometime in the early 2000s. I tell you this to give you hope that unhealthy cycles of conflict can be stopped, reversed, and replaced with better ways of handling frustration. But first we must figure out why conflict begins and what to do when it does.

In many ongoing relationships, especially close relationships, unhealthy patterns of relating can easily become the norm. This is problematic when you consider that relationships don't usually disintegrate in one explosive moment of conflict. More commonly, relationships erode over time, as we keep circling around the same issues and peace is chipped away, bit by bit.

On the fateful day JP and I got off our crazy conflict cycle, we stumbled onto the reason for our conflict and the resulting remedy by accident (and probably some divine intervention from the Holy Spirit).

We'd had another blowup. I stood at the kitchen sink looking out the window into the backyard, where JP begrudgingly repaired a sprinkler. On one hand, I felt defeated over our interaction, but on the other hand, I was delighted I'd no longer have to endure patches of brown grass. Suddenly, I became aware of our conflict pattern. Before that day, I'd never paused long enough to objectively consider our interactions. Our arguments just *happened*. Or so it seemed.

In reality, our ongoing battles over household chores weren't random at all; they were quite predictable. We'd adopted the ask, ignore, nag, explode pattern—a common archetype for spouses, parents, and bosses. The insidious nature of this pattern is that while it creates relational chaos, it also produces results. Which, of course, is why we use it.

You know what I'm talking about, don't you? You tell your child to clean his room, do his homework, or put down his cell phone, and if he doesn't immediately comply, the ask, ignore, nag, explode cycle is triggered.

Or maybe a coworker rarely gets paperwork in on time—cue the ask, ignore, nag, explode cycle. Or your sibling doesn't follow through on a promise to help with your aging parent, or . . . you get the picture.

Not all destructive conflict cycles follow this precise pattern. Some cycles involve avoidance, silent treatments, guilt trips, tears, pouty behavior, slammed doors, or, in extreme cases, physical or emotional abuse. However, ongoing battles almost always exhibit common themes and repeated behaviors. When you step back and pause long enough to look, you'll see them.

That's what happened to me on that warm spring Saturday in a personal aha moment of clarity. My newfound insight about the *why* behind our arguments deflated every ounce of anger I had, so I ventured out to the yard and sat down on the grass beside my husband.

JP continued to work, but he glanced up long enough to signal he'd listen if I had something to say.

"I figured out why we always argue about stuff like this," I said, pointing to the sprinklers. "We're stuck in a pattern." JP looked confused until I explained my epiphany.

When I finished, JP nodded in agreement. He saw our pattern too. But he added one last piece of information that turned out to be crucial.

"You know, Donna, I really do have good intentions when it comes to fixing stuff around the house, but I bet you aren't aware of the timing when you ask."

Now I was the one confused. "What do you mean?"

"Typically, you ask me to fix something at the end of the day.

It's not that I don't want to do what you ask. I just don't want to do it *then*. And, because it's late and I'm tired, I easily forget."

I mentally scrolled through my most recent requests and had to admit he was right. Frankly, I couldn't blame him for not wanting to fix a sprinkler or door hinge at ten o'clock at night. Heck, I wouldn't want to either.

"So, what should we do to make it a win for both of us?" I asked.

"How about if you keep a running list of projects you'd like me to do around the house, along with the dates the projects need to be completed? That way you don't have to feel like you're continually asking, and I have flexibility about when things get done."

This was the moment we ended our crazy conflict cycle, at least as it related to household chores. Looking back, here's what we did that helped.

1. IDENTIFY REPEATED ISSUES

Repeated issues are easy to spot. Look for the arguments that happen consistently—battles over homework; sibling squabbles over borrowed clothes, toys, or tech; meltdowns at dinnertime or bedtime; differences over how to spend money, what to do with free time, frequency of sex, household responsibilities, where to spend the holidays; and so on. If you notice an argument about a single matter more than three times, you've likely encountered a repeated issue.

2. IDENTIFY REPEATED PATTERNS

Call me crazy, but this is the fun part. Once you've identified a repeated issue, your mission is to simply observe how the dispute is handled. If you're really self-restrained, you can do this in the moment of conflict. Most of us, though, need time to reflect on what was said, what was done, and in what order. We play the role of detective so we can pinpoint what's defective. Note that we're not looking for what's defective in the other person ("They're selfish, judgmental, overly sensitive, controlling, and impossible to deal with!"). And we're not looking for what's defective in us ("I'm a loser, a doormat, a nag, a pushover, or a control freak"). Instead, we are looking for what's defective in the interaction itself.

3. COLLABORATE TO FIND A WIN-WIN SOLUTION

Once we identify repeated issues and repeated patterns, it's time to work together to find solutions. The best way to open the door for collaboration is to start with common ground or common feelings. Functionally, this allows each party to acknowledge one portion of the problem, essentially conceding, "Yep, I see it that way too." They can agree on the frustration, even if they don't agree on the facts surrounding the frustration. At this point, the collaboration continues with a simple question, such as "What do you think is the best way to handle our dilemma?" or "How can this issue be a win for you and a win for me?" Admittedly, we can't always find a win-win, but in many cases, we can come close.

Here are some examples of how these conversations can look:

- "I realize I've been a nag, and honestly, I hate that side of me. I'm guessing you don't like it much either."
- "Have you noticed there's a lot of fighting surrounding

homework? I don't want to yell at you every night, and I'm pretty sure you'd like things better if I didn't yell at you either. Is that right?"

- "Because I care about you, I hate all the tension in our relationship. Do you feel the tension too?"
- "I've noticed we seem to go around and around about the same issue, which probably frustrates you as much as it does me."

For JP and me, the collaboration to find a win-win over our ongoing battle of household repairs put us in a position to either work it out or suffer the ongoing headache of relational conflict. (By the way, if you're thinking, *Why didn't she just hire someone to fix stuff?* the short answer is we couldn't afford to at that point in our lives.) We chose to work it out, and learning to do so matured us. We became stronger and wiser both as individuals and as a couple.

It's worth noting that our strategy worked because we both stuck to our game plan. If one or both of us hadn't followed through—if I'd never written down what needed to be fixed or if JP had failed to fix things I'd written down—anger and deep resentment would almost certainly have developed.

And, in many cases, this is *exactly* what happens. One or both parties fail to follow through.

Even if they have good intentions to do so.

Here's the reality: relationship progress is often two steps forward, one step back, especially where conflict is concerned. Just when we think an issue is resolved—*bam!*—it comes careening back into our life. Patterns don't often change overnight.

This is where accountability, boundaries, and consequences come in. But it's also at this point that we must return to the foundational fact that we cannot coerce another person to change; we can only change ourselves.

Yes, we can provide the motivation and the context for change, but we cannot *force* change; that's called being controlling. Remember the root cause of human conflict? The one my professor at UCLA taught us?

PATTERNS DON'T OFTEN CHANGE OVERNIGHT.

All human conflict is really about control.

Which means, in the heat of the battle, we must ask ourselves questions like "Am I trying to control this person or maintain a connection with this person?" Our endgame matters.

Sometimes gaining control of chaos is necessary. For instance, parents certainly need to rein in out-of-control kids, and employers sometimes need to regain control of an out-of-control work environment. But control is healthy only to the extent that it helps connection to continue. Control isn't always bad, but *being controlling* is.

How can we tell if we're trying to maintain control or if we're being controlling? Ask yourself (and be honest): *Do I want to please myself, or do I genuinely want to please God?*

The real answer regarding our motivations always shows up in our behavior. A little self-assessment goes a long way in determining what drives us. We can ask ourselves: *If I don't get what I want, do I throw a fit, yell, pout, blame, play the victim, or use the silent treatment? Do I emotionally check out or physically walk out? Do I name-call, talk about people behind their back, or resort to violence?* If the answer is yes to any of these questions, we're being controlling. If we allow other people to do these things to us, we're being controlled.

Let's return to the crazy conflict cycle JP and I found ourselves in. Every time I nagged, and every time I exploded, I felt justified. My thought process went something like this: *If he'd just do what I asked, when I asked, I'd never nag him and never explode.* (It's amazing what a nice person I can be if everyone just does what I want them to do when I want them to do it!)

Underneath this thought was the notion that JP was to blame for my behavior.

But was he?

Here's where control gets wonky and unhealthy: if I think your behavior is to blame for my behavior, I feel justified in trying to control your behavior. In other words, if you stop your actions, I can stop mine—hence my desire to tell you: "Stop your actions!" But since we can never force another person to change, the conflict-control cycle is the thing that's *actually* out of control.

The good news is that we can get off the crazy conflict-control cycle when we learn to communicate and cooperate. But in order to do this, it helps to know the real reason behind our anger.

WHY DO WE GET ANGRY ANYWAY?

Anger stems from one of three sources: blocked goals, unmet desires, or perceived wrongs. Let's take a look at what each of these can look like.

1. BLOCKED GOALS

Think about all the times unforeseen traffic has made you late. Were you irritated? Ever wonder why? Your goal to be on time was blocked by something (traffic) you couldn't control.

How about the moments when your kids argued but you needed

to get work done? Did you get angry? Probably. Their bickering blocked your goal.

What about the time when the homeowners' association made you resubmit your plans? Or when your coworker didn't pull their weight so the team didn't make quota? Or when you were put on hold for an hour waiting for a customer service rep to take your call? Blocked goal. Blocked goal. Blocked goal.

This is not to say that anger is always an inappropriate response. (Remember Ephesians 4:26: "In your anger do not sin.") This simply explains one reason we get angry in the first place.

2. UNMET DESIRES

What about unmet desires?

Interestingly, the Bible speaks directly about the role desires play in conflict: "What causes fights and quarrels among you? Don't they come from your desires that battle within you?" (James 4:1).

Unmet desires triggered my anger with JP, and they triggered his anger with me. I had a desire to keep our home a lovely place in working order, but brown patches of grass and doors falling off kitchen cabinets do not a lovely home make. JP had a desire for rest at the end of a long, demanding workday, but home repairs and honey-do lists don't make the cut for "things to do to unwind." Our unmet desires sparked frustration, which eventually led to anger.

What made our scenario more challenging was my desire moved in direct opposition of his desire. (Correct me if I'm wrong, but I think this is called "real life.")

In his book *The Peacemaker*, Ken Sande wrote:

> Unmet desires have the potential of working themselves deeper
> and deeper into our hearts. This is especially true when we come

to see a desire as something we need or deserve and therefore must have in order to be happy or fulfilled. . . . The trouble is that if these seemingly legitimate desires are not met, we can find ourselves in a vicious cycle. The more we want something, the more we think we need and deserve it. And the more we think we are entitled to something, the more convinced we are that we cannot be happy and secure without it.

When we see something as being essential to our fulfillment and well-being, it moves from being a desire to a demand. "I wish I could have this" evolves into "I must have this!" This is where trouble sets in. Even if the initial desire was not inherently wrong, it has grown so strong that it begins to control our thoughts and behavior.[1]

When an unmet desire begins to control our thoughts and behavior, conflict is virtually guaranteed.

So we've seen how blocked goals and unmet desires contribute to anger, but what about perceived wrongs?

3. PERCEIVED WRONGS

A perceived wrong is anything someone else says or does that we believe to be unkind, unethical, immoral, or unbiblical. These words or actions don't have to *be* wrong in order to generate anger; we just need to perceive that they are wrong.

For instance, if your spouse makes a comment he intended as a lighthearted joke but to you it seems hurtful and embarrassing, you've encountered a "perceived wrong" and will likely feel anger in addition to embarrassment or hurt. This isn't to say perceived wrongs can't actually *be* wrong; sometimes they are. The point, though, is how the strong feeling of anger rises inside of us whether the wrong is real *or* merely perceived.

When our anger stems from a perceived wrong, we often say things like "That's not fair!" "That's not right!" "How could they do that?" or "This is all my fault. I'm a terrible person." Unhealthy methods of coping with perceived wrongs include putting all the blame on another person or, conversely, placing all the blame on oneself. Further, the angered or hurt person often fails to consider that the conflict could simply be a result of miscommunication or misinterpretation. Of course, sometimes blame does reside with one party, but in most day-to-day conflict drama, each person contributes at least a little.

MOVING FROM WHY YOU'RE ANGRY TO WHAT TO DO NEXT

If we want the conflict cycle to end, we must put a stake in the ground and decide to stop it. Few relationships—personal or professional—can be sustained over prolonged periods of intense conflict, whether the conflict manifests itself in aggressive behavior (screaming, shouting, or blaming) or passive behavior (pouting, silent treatments, and scowling).

The longer we keep circling around the same issues, using the same destructive patterns, the higher the probability the relationship will disintegrate—either actively, when one person leaves physically, or passively, when one person leaves emotionally. When unhealthy patterns aren't reversed, someone will walk out or check out. This is true in families ("I was out the door the minute I turned eighteen!"),

WHEN UNHEALTHY PATTERNS AREN'T REVERSED, SOMEONE WILL WALK OUT OR CHECK OUT.

in businesses ("The turnover rate there is through the roof!"), and even in places of worship ("The church just split!").

If we want to make regret-free choices in the midst of real-life conflict, it's vital to understand where our anger comes from, identify repeated issues and repeated patterns, and communicate about these issues in a spirit of cooperation.

That's where we're going next.

Lord, I want out of the crazy conflict cycle! Open my eyes to see repeated issues and repeated patterns, as well as my destructive rather than constructive ways of relating. Help me live aware of the source of my anger. Alert me when I'm being controlling. Help me, instead, to be self-controlled because I'm filled up with You. May the fruit of Your Spirit be always evident in me. Show me where a desire has become a demand—or worse, an idol. Teach me new patterns of relating, ones that demonstrate Your grace and better align my relationships to reflect You and Your love, amen.

PUTTING PEACE INTO PRACTICE

1. Can you identify a conflict cycle in any of your relationships— with a spouse, child, family member, or friend? If so, what is the repeated issue? What is the repeated pattern? (What do you typically do or say, and what do they typically do or say?)

2. How do you think God wants you to alter this cycle? Try to be specific.

3. Review your most recent feelings of anger. Was the anger generated by a blocked goal, an unmet desire, a perceived wrong, or a combination of the three? Pause right now and talk to God about the root of your anger. Write down anything you think God wants to teach you about this root.

4. I discussed the difference between maintaining a sense of control and being controlling. Can you spot any way you've been controlling with others? Have you allowed yourself to be controlled in any way?

5. Are you in a relationship where a destructive pattern, if not reversed, could eventually lead to the relationship's disintegration? Ask God for wisdom in dealing with these circumstances.

SIX

SHOULD I BE MAD?
BIG THINGS, SMALL THINGS,
AND EVERYTHING IN BETWEEN

Not all conflicts are equal.

Let that truth sink in for a moment.

Some of us find it easy to spiral over the smallest infractions: The dishwasher didn't get loaded. The in-laws treated the kids to ice cream an hour before dinner. Our spouse buys us an unwanted birthday gift. Our sister doesn't call back the same afternoon we call her. Our neighbor keeps his garbage cans out overnight. Our adult child visits for two days rather than the expected three.

Others of us let small things go, but we prefer to sweep major irritations and infractions under the rug. People who fall into this camp think, *Perhaps if I ignore the problem, it will go away.* These folks have lived with the proverbial elephant in the room so long they might as well buy him a bed and cook him meals.

Since all conflict is not equal, all responses to conflict should

DON'T MAKE THE SMALL THINGS BIG, BUT DON'T MAKE THE BIG THINGS SMALL.

not be equal either. The key to handling conflict wisely is this: don't make the small things big, but don't make the big things small.

Our tendency, however, is to do the opposite. We magnify small irritations and minimize major infractions. People who manage conflict in regret-free ways learn to discern the difference between big things and small things and handle each appropriately. The challenge, of course, is to properly identify a big thing versus a small thing.

SMALL THINGS

Molly is halfway through making dessert for the Bible study she and her husband, Brad, are scheduled to attend when she realizes she's out of eggs. Molly glances at the clock to check the time. *Perfect. Brad can stop at the grocery store on his way home.* Molly picks up her phone and sends Brad a text.

"Hey babe! Would you mind stopping at the store before you come home? We're out of eggs and I need them to make the cake for small group."

"Sure, no problem."

An hour later Brad walks into the house with three bags of groceries. As he and Molly unload the bags, which are stuffed with the kind of junk food Molly never buys, Molly notices something missing: eggs.

"Brad, where are the eggs?"

Brad looks sheepish. "I guess I got sidetracked and forgot the eggs."

In this moment, Molly has a choice. What she says and what she does next will affect her personal peace and the peace she experiences with her spouse.

What does Molly do?

a. Berate Brad with guilt and shame comments. She says, "You never listen! You're such a child. I ask one little favor of you, and you can't even handle it."

b. Play the martyr, saying, "I guess I have to do everything around here!"

c. Storm out of the kitchen with a scowl on her face. Then she goes to the grocery store herself.

d. Punish Brad by refusing to speak to him as they drive to their small group.

e. Say to Brad, "It's frustrating to know I can't count on you when you say you'll do something I asked. Now we'll probably be late, which makes me stressed. Honestly, I'm angry."

f. Hand Brad the car keys with a smile and say, "Well, since you need to go back for eggs, you might as well get bread too. On second thought, maybe just get the eggs."

Every conflict is a multiple-choice test. We have options. Make the best choice, and we experience relational peace. Make the worst choice, and we experience relational pain.

Proverbs 19:11 says, "Good sense makes one slow to anger, and it is his glory to overlook an offense" (ESV). Sometimes it's easy to spot small matters we should overlook. Other times, though, it's more difficult to discern the difference between issues that should be overlooked and issues that should be addressed.

How do we know whether we should overlook an offense? We overlook an offense if it fits at least one of the following:

1. It's a one-time occurrence.
2. It doesn't have ongoing consequences.
3. It doesn't damage the relationship or the people in the relationship.

Let's look at Molly and Brad's situation considering these three filters. Is Brad's mistake a one-time occurrence? If so, it's probably best to laugh it off or focus more on how to get the eggs than how to make Brad pay for not getting the eggs. A one-time occurrence rarely bears long-term consequences (though there are exceptions— more on that later). Conflicts without ongoing consequences don't usually damage the relationship or the people in the relationship. Therefore, for Molly, the benefit of overlooking the offense outweighs the benefit of addressing the offense.

Looking back at Molly's choices, I'd recommend option *f.* The best multiple-choice answer for many of life's day-to-day conflicts can be summed up in three words: *Let. It. Go.*

But what if this is not a one-time occurrence? What if Brad's made a similar mistake in the past? Molly will want to address the issue without making matters worse, which means no shameful comments, name-calling, martyrdom, or punishment. Therefore, option *e* is the best choice. Brad's forgetfulness is frustrating, for sure, but it's probably not a fatal flaw, which means it's still a "small thing."

It's important to note that not all three filters must be present for us to overlook an offense. For instance, some irritations and disagreements happen repeatedly, but they're still small things. An example of a repeated small thing is a spouse, roommate, or child who's not as tidy as we'd prefer. In the grand scheme of life, tidiness—or lack of it—is generally a small thing, much like a spouse's occasional forgetfulness.

In our earlier years of marriage, JP had a habit where sometime in the night, every night, he'd take off his T-shirt and throw it on the bedroom floor next to our bed. At the time, JP left for work at dark o'clock, while I was still asleep. Each morning I'd wake to see his T-shirt lying on the floor.

My thought process went something like this: *Why do I have to be the one to pick up his T-shirt? He's a grown man, for heaven's sake! On top of that, he's on his way to our closet where we keep the laundry basket. Would it be so hard for him to pick up his own shirt? Am I this family's personal maid? Blah, blah, blah . . .*

This went on for months—years, maybe. The daily thought was so brief, I honestly didn't pay much attention to it. Until one morning when I paused long enough to notice it.

Listen to yourself. You're being ridiculous. You start your day mad at your husband over a T-shirt left on the floor. Really? That's going to be your big issue? You have a loving, hardworking husband who's a great dad and a godly man, and this is what you focus on? Seriously? Girl, get a grip and make a change!

So I did. From that day on, whenever I picked up JP's T-shirt, I held it to my chest and prayed for him as I walked from our bed to the hamper.

Overlooking this repeated small offense not only brought me peace, but it produced a harvest of peace in our marriage too. This is why the Bible tells us it is a glory to overlook an offense.

What is your current "T-shirt on the floor" or "I forgot the eggs" issue? If you're in relationship with people, you likely have one. Is there one small thing God is whispering to your heart, saying, "You'll have more peace and less regret if you don't make that small thing big"?

BIG THINGS

Wise people don't make small things big, but neither do they make big things small. Big things are never best ignored. How do you know if an issue is a big thing?

1. It's a repeated occurrence.
2. It will have ongoing negative consequences.
3. It will damage the relationship or the people in the relationship.

God's Word tells us, "Be angry and do not sin" (Ephesians 4:26 ESV). Did you know there are some issues where the *godliest* response is anger? I realize this might not jibe with your current perspective on conflict. This "being angry" business could be contrary to what you've been taught—specifically, that being angry doesn't seem very Christian. Perhaps being angry is something you believe "nice people" don't do. You may even be thinking, *Wait a minute. Didn't Jesus tell us to "turn the other cheek"?*

Yet there it is, smack-dab in the middle of Ephesians 4: "Be angry."

Of course, the verse goes on to say "do not sin." Sinful anger is anger that "focuses on punishing the *offender* rather than the moral content of the *offense.*"[1] What we get angry about and how we handle our anger determines whether it's helpful or hurtful, sinful or sanctified.

Pause right here. Reread the previous sentence, focusing on two words: *helpful* and *sanctified*. If the result of our anger and how we deal with said anger helps the relationship become healthier and helps the people in the relationship become sanctified, anger is a righteous response.

Remember, anger is an emotion, *not an action*. Many of us equate anger with sin because we've experienced the devastating effects of actions born from the emotion. However—and this is key—it's possible to divorce sinful, hurtful actions from the emotion and marry the human emotion of anger with helpful responses, ones that promote relational healing. This is the message of Ephesians 4:26: "In your anger do not sin."

For those of us who are uncomfortable addressing the elephant in the room by confronting sin, we must learn to embrace anger as a righteous response to real wrongs. It's unwise to confuse the commands to forgive, be submissive, or love one another with free passes for those who do us, or others, harm.

Dishonesty, disrespect, adultery, addiction, and abuse are a few big things that must not be swept under the rug. Ever. If you struggle to address big issues like these, ask for help. There is no shame in admitting a big issue is big. Heavy issues are often too weighty to shoulder ourselves. We need others for support, wisdom, guidance, and prayer.

Big issues aren't always watershed behaviors like addiction, abuse, dishonesty, or disrespect. Sometimes small annoyances can become big things, especially if failing to address them will harm the relationship over time. To help weigh the gravity of a conflict, we must bear in mind the long-term effects it will have on the people involved and the health of their relationship. When seemingly "small things" persist enough to damage relationships, they fall into the "big things" category and should be addressed.

Admittedly, it often feels easier to ignore some issues, especially when we fear pushback. Few of us like to bring up concerns when it would be easier to overlook behavior and "keep the peace." But every big relational issue we address *now* prevents us from experiencing the fallout of big relational consequences *later*.

Margo, the manager of a large company, is known for her personal, professional, yet easygoing nature. She hires only qualified people she trusts and doesn't micromanage their day-to-day responsibilities, though she gives appropriate oversight. Most of her employees have worked for her for years. Why wouldn't they? She's a dream manager!

Over the years one employee distinguished himself with his exceptional work and charming personality. He asked for more responsibility, and Margo promoted him. There was just one small problem with this employee: he never asked Margo; he *told* Margo. At first this showed up in the way he failed to ask for days off; he just informed Margo of his plans. This repeated behavior bothered Margo a bit, but since his work ethic was never in question, Margo let it go. Her easygoing nature didn't lend itself to making an issue over things she deemed minor. However, over time, Margo noticed other things too. He began to want more input into Margo's responsibilities, but he resisted anyone giving input into his responsibilities. Eventually, Margo learned he made a play for her job and wanted her gone. What was once a pleasant place to work had now become a cesspool of office politics and pressure.

Looking back, Margo says she regrets not addressing the seemingly small thing that was actually a big thing. She wishes she'd paid more attention to repeated issues instead of dismissing them as "no big deal." She wonders if she'd addressed her concerns early on if their working relationship might have been different.

As we move forward in our quest of healthier relationships, more peace, and less stressed-filled conflict, it's vital to understand that *peacekeeping* is not the same as *peacemaking*. On occasion it will be necessary to disrupt what presents as peace but isn't. Only then can we trade the counterfeit peace we've settled for with the authentic peace we long for.

Big issues always bear big consequences—if not now, eventually. Therefore, just as we must determine not to make small things big, we must also determine not to make big things small.

EVERYTHING IN BETWEEN

We began this chapter with the goal of answering the question "Should I be mad?" So far, we've seen that most small things aren't worth arguing about, and most big issues aren't worth ignoring. But what about the in-between parts of human relationships? How do we deal with those?

SURFACE ISSUES VERSUS REAL ISSUES

A surface issue is what a conflict *appears* to be about. A real issue is what a conflict is *actually* about. If we argue about surface issues, peace will forever elude us; but if we address the real issues, peace has a chance to be found.

One oft-overlooked real-versus-surface issue is an argument's physical component. You, like me, have probably had countless ridiculous arguments when the real issue is that one or both parties is stressed, late, hungry, tired, hormonal, or in chronic pain. If we argue with a child who's tired, a teen who's hungry, a spouse who's sick, or a coworker who's stressed, we'll almost certainly be arguing over surface issues rather than real issues.

Sometimes the solution to conflict is so simple we stumble right over it: Feed the child. Put the toddler down for a nap. Pick up the slack for a family member who's ill. Overlook a stressed-out co-worker's abruptness. Give grace to the teen with PMS. Don't bring up a heavy topic with a spouse, roommate, or child first thing in the morning or late at night.

If we ask ourselves, *Is there an unmet physical or emotional need that's contributing to the conflict?* we'll often discover a simple solution to what, at first, appeared to be a complex conflict.

Occasionally we'll need to ask ourselves this same question about our own reactions because anger is a thermometer.

When our relationships clip along seamlessly, our thermometer stays cool. However, with each relational hiccup, the temperature rises just a bit.

Think about your typical day. It may involve challenges with kids, conversations with coworkers, conflicting goals with clients, caustic strangers, incompetent customer service representatives, or a cranky spouse. One of these things will raise our emotional temperature a degree or two. But combine several of these challenges, and our emotional mercury is sent soaring.

Soon our capacity to stay calm has nearly reached the top of our emotional thermometer. One small thing—something we'd otherwise deem minor—can easily cause us to blow our top. Or completely blow up the relationship.

Either way, the outcome leaves us hanging our head in shame and guilt.

What does this mean for us as we seek to navigate conflict in a God-honoring way in all the "in-between" areas of life?

1. We pay attention to small, incremental increases in frustration. It's almost impossible to live with self-control if we live without self-awareness.

2. We invite God into our emotions. This is where prayer comes in. We might pray something like this: *God, I can feel my frustration growing. Open my eyes to see why this is happening and give me wisdom to handle things Your way.*

3. We actively look for ways to lower our emotional temperature. Taking a walk, listening to worship music, and calling a friend who makes us laugh or listens well can rein in skyrocketing emotions and lower the temperature back into normal range.

4. When we feel our emotional temperature rising, we can let others know where we stand in terms of our capacity to handle additional stress. Try saying, "On an emotional temperature scale of 1 to 100, I'm at about a 99.5." Conflict with a person whose anger-meter registers 99.5 will almost certainly be more about surface issues than real issues.

Once we know there's no underlying unmet emotional or physical need that could prevent us from dealing with real issues, we're in a prime position to discern what to do next. It can be helpful to have a category in which to place the conflict at hand. In my experience, conflict comes in one of three forms.

Conflict #1: Irritations. Irritations almost always fall into the "small things" category. Irritations are habits, words, or behaviors that grate on our nerves, frustrate us, or bother us. Some personality types and behaviors rub us the wrong way, even if we can't pinpoint why. It's not that these things are wrong or sinful; they're merely distinct, contrasting ways of doing life.

- Messy versus neat
- Fast versus slow

- Talkative versus quiet
- Take-charge versus laid-back
- High-maintenance versus low-maintenance
- Decisive versus indecisive
- Internal processing versus external processing

What do each of these pairs have in common? They are differences. Different does not equal wrong; different is just . . . different.

But, boy, different can irritate us to the point of being irate, can't it?

Countless unwarranted arguments have their genesis in irritation. For instance, a decisive person loses their patience with an indecisive person ("Come on, already! Make a decision!"); a low-maintenance person judges a high-maintenance person ("Why are you so picky about how your food is prepared? You're so difficult! It's embarrassing."); or an external processor pressures an internal processor ("We need to resolve this right now!"), and the internal processor snaps back ("Get off my back. You never give me time to think!"). These are just a few examples that illustrate how irritations can drive us to the point of irateness if we let them.

However, since irritations are usually about *our preferences* and not someone else's problem, it's up to us to overlook small behaviors that bug us.

Conflict #2: Insults. A second conflict category is insults. When a family member tells a joke at our expense, a spouse or child speaks to us disrespectfully, or we bear the brunt of a coworker's snide comment (or we do any of these things to others), we've encountered an insult. Insults also include name-calling, sarcastic remarks, and slander. *Any* word or deed that tears another down is an insult.

Years ago I stopped into a local mini-mart to purchase a bottle of water, and a woman with several middle-school-age kids—six boys and one girl, to be exact—walked in after me. The woman appeared to be the carpool mom on after-school pickup duty. And she was *frazzled*.

"Stop touching that.

"Slow down.

"You kids are driving me nuts."

As I watched the scene unfold, I noticed the lone girl was calm and the boys were rowdy, but not overly so. In fact, the boys were respectful, even with their energy. The kids were just being *kids*.

I grabbed my cold drink and headed to the counter to pay, where the mom and the teenage girl, who was the woman's spitting image, also waited.

"Would you boys settle down? You kids are animals! I don't know why I bothered to bring you in here!" hissed the mom under her breath, but still loud enough for me to hear.

The daughter looked eagerly at her mother, clearly seeking affirmation and approval. "I'm not like them, am I, Mom?"

Time seemed to stand still as the mother turned to face her daughter, with a look that could only be described as disdain.

"You? Ha! You're worse than all the boys put together!"

Then the mom rolled her eyes in disgust but turned away just in time to miss what I witnessed: the crestfallen face of an insulted child.

Sadly, scenarios like this play out every day in homes, businesses, schools, and neighborhoods. Maybe even yours.

Have you ever heard comments like these?

- "I have three kids. Four if you count my husband."
- "She's such a drama queen."

- "He's a lazy bum."
- "How can you be so dumb?"
- "You're a loser."
- "Why can't you be more like your sister?"
- "You'll never amount to anything."

If you've heard any of these comments, or ones like them, you've been in the presence of an insult.

Insults *always* injure.

Since insults damage people and relationships, insults fall into the "big things" category.

So how do we deal with insults lobbed at us—or worse, insults we've lobbed at others?

If we've insulted someone, we must admit that our natural, fleshly tendency is to justify insults with excuses. For example: "I was stressed out," "I didn't really mean it," "She drove me to it," or "He had it coming." But if we try to excuse words that wound another person, we're effectively saying, "I'm unwilling to take responsibility for my behavior and my part in our relationship drama. I don't really care about you. I care about me."

Long-term peace and relational reconciliation are never possible for people who do not take personal responsibility for their words and actions. Therefore, if we insult another person, it's our responsibility to recognize the damage we've done, humble ourselves, and ask for forgiveness. The correct response if we insult someone is heartfelt: "My words hurt you. I was wrong. I am sorry."

One word of caution: many people feel insulted or offended by the slightest word, look, or action. If you fall into the "easily offended" category, you'll need to humbly admit your propensity to being overly sensitive. (Come on. You can be honest here. This is a safe space for learning how to handle conflict better so you can find more peace.)

Sometimes what feels like an insult may not actually be an insult.

Being overly sensitive is as big a contributor to relational disharmony as being insensitive to others' feelings. Sometimes personal sensitivity is born from personal insecurity. If you realize you get your feelings hurt often, you're likely placing unrealistic expectations on others. When this happens, others may feel manipulated by your emotions ("We have to do things Mom's way; you know how she gets if we don't"). Or others may think, *No matter how hard I try, I can never do enough. With her, I can't win for losing.*

Instead of drawing others in, the easily offended person drives others away. They may win the conflict, but they lose the closeness they desperately desire. As a result, being easily offended makes relational harmony hard and personal peace practically impossible to maintain.

If you're easily offended, try asking yourself two questions the next time you feel offended:

1. Did this person *intend* to hurt me with their words or actions?
2. Am I offended because I feel insecure in some way?

Sometimes we label other people's words as *insults* when we should label our feelings as *insecure*.

Conflict #3: Issues. At first glance, issues appear to be the most difficult conflict category to solve; however, sometimes they are the easiest. Examples of common marriage issues include how we spend our money, how we discipline the kids, or how we spend free time. In friendship, issues might be who initiates with whom, how often, and when. In parenting, issues can be things like homework, household chores, curfews, or screen time.

The key to solving an issue is this: keep the problem the problem; don't make the person the problem.

An issue becomes complicated when we become irritated at the way another person handles the issue. Irritation can easily morph into insults. If we allow our irritation to lead us to insult, we make the person the problem instead.

Whenever we make a person the problem, we approach the issue as "you against me." But when we keep the problem the problem, we approach the issue as "you and me against the problem."

Take Jen and Marcus, who battled over their finances for years. Marcus was a spender while Jen was a saver, which meant they had different approaches to money. These differences quickly led to irritations, and their irritations led to insults.

"Why did you buy that? Do you think money grows on trees?"

"You're such a spoilsport. You used to be so much fun, but now all you do is nag."

"Well, someone has to be the responsible one around here, and it's obviously not you!"

On and on they'd go. One insult followed by another, followed by another. Conflict became their constant companion. To make matters worse, their financial issue never got resolved but, much like their insults, became more intense over time. Their story was a living, breathing example of Galatians 5:15: "If you bite and devour each other, watch out or you will be destroyed by each other."

Until they stopped making the person the problem and started making the problem the problem.

Jen and Marcus both wanted to live comfortably within their means; on this one thing they could agree. Of course, Marcus focused more on the "comfortably" part, while Jen gravitated to the "within their means" part. Still, they both admitted the idea of decreasing their conflict while simultaneously achieving their goal seemed appealing.

Jen and Marcus tackled their problem by *first* identifying their individual interests, then focusing on one interest they both shared.

Author and reconciliation specialist Ken Sande explained the importance of considering interests in conflict resolution, once again in his book *The Peacemaker*:

> A *position* is a desired outcome or a definable perspective on an issue. For example: "If the dog keeps barking, you should get rid of her," or "She's my dog, and you have no right to tell me what to do with her."
>
> An *interest* is what motivates people. It is a concern, desire, need, limitation, or something a person values. Interests provide the basis for positions. . . . When people focus on interests rather than positions, it is usually easier to develop acceptable solutions.[2]

The most effective conflict resolvers start by identifying a common interest. If you're unsure about another person's interest (or you're unsure of your own), listen for phrases like these: "What I really want is . . ." or "It's important to me that . . ." or "I wish . . ." Such phrases indicate wants and desires, or, as Sande dubbed them, "interests." An interest can range from "I'd like us to remain friends" to "I want to feel respected at work" to "I need your dog to stop barking all day."

Most conflict negotiations go sideways when we fail to consider others' interests and focus solely on our own interests. As fundamental as this sounds, it's reality: few people are motivated by giving us what *we* want; most humans are motivated by getting what *they* want. If we launch into why someone should give us what we want without considering what they want, our effort at conflict resolution is doomed from the start.

Notice how Jen and Marcus started with a shared interest: less conflict while living comfortably within their means. Up to this point Jen focused only on her interest (saving money to feel secure), while Marcus focused solely on his interest (spending money as enjoyment). As a result, their problem remained a problem.

If we fail to understand another's interests—what motivates them, and what they desire—we'll almost always fail to find a workable solution. However, if we broach a problem saying, "How can I make this a win for you, not just a win for me?" the likelihood of resolving conflict in the best interests of all parties is increased. Problems get solved and relationships get preserved. Everyone experiences more peace and less regret.

So, armed with the knowledge of their common interest, Jen and Marcus sat down at their kitchen table one warm summer evening, took out a piece of paper, and wrote these words across the top: "The Problem: Find a Way for Jen and Marcus to Both Live Comfortably Without Overspending."

Writing a problem on paper clarifies the issue. Doing so makes problems objective rather than subjective, concrete rather than abstract. Writing a problem places it "out there" instead of on a spin cycle inside our brains.

After writing out the problem, Marcus and Jen laid a few ground rules: No insults. No dismissing a suggestion. No eye rolls, loud sighs, or other nonverbal indications that an idea was stupid or impractical. Their purpose was solely to brainstorm options that had even the remotest possibility of helping both partners live comfortably without overspending.

Then they bowed their heads and asked God to direct their thoughts and their conversation. They knew they'd need God's help to succeed where they'd so often failed before. This was new territory for Marcus and Jen. They'd never handled a problem this way, and it felt strangely unfamiliar, yet pleasantly hopeful.

After Jen and Marcus brainstormed, they looked at their list. Right away a few suggestions were untenable to both, so they crossed those off the list. A few more ideas were dismissed if either Marcus or Jen felt uncomfortable because they seemed too restrictive or too lenient. At this point, tensions began to mount—old habits die hard—but both Jen and Marcus resisted the temptation to turn on each other. Instead, they kept their attention on solving the problem with their common interests in mind.

Finally, Marcus took the lead. "Would it make you feel more comfortable if I didn't spend more than $250 unless I talked to you first?"

Jen could hardly believe her ears. "Wow. Yes, that would really help."

Marcus's humility and willingness to bend prompted Jen to do the same. She'd never considered a compromise in the past—it felt too risky—but now it came naturally.

"You know what? I'd still feel okay if the number were a little higher, and that way you'd have more flexibility. What do you think?"

"Yeah. That'd be great."

For the first time in their married life, Jen and Marcus went to bed at peace after discussing their finances. And all they did was keep the problem the problem instead of making the person the problem.

I realize Marcus and Jen's story may sound simplistic. Not all issues can be resolved in one kitchen-table meeting. But some issues can. Frankly, for those of us who endure constant conflict, some peace rather than no peace would be a welcome relief.

But there's another benefit to keeping the problem the problem: even when a problem centers around a person—such as when addiction or dishonesty is involved—the real problem is still not the person but rather *how to deal* with the addiction, *how to rebuild* trust, *how to respond* to the person in a way that sets the relationship up for the best possible outcome.

People have problems, and people cause problems, but people aren't problems.

> PEOPLE HAVE PROBLEMS, AND PEOPLE CAUSE PROBLEMS, BUT PEOPLE AREN'T PROBLEMS.

Yes, other people must do their part to solve their problems, and when they don't, new problems will arise. Often this means we have to put boundaries in place; almost always it means there will be relational consequences. Still, we can't resolve a person; we can only resolve a problem. When faced with an issue that causes conflict, the best course of action is to keep the problem the problem and resist the temptation to make the person the problem.

INTENTIONAL OFFENSES VERSUS UNINTENTIONAL OFFENSES

One last piece of the conflict puzzle can help us determine when to overlook an offense versus when to address an offense.

Just as not all conflicts are equal, not all motivations behind conflict are equal either. If an offender didn't mean to hurt us, anger us, disrespect us, or demean us, and if the behavior is not an on-going problem, it's best to overlook an offense. After all, who among us hasn't said something and afterward thought, *That came out the wrong way. What if the person misunderstood me?* Who among us hasn't cancelled a commitment, forgotten a friend's birthday, or done some other dumb thing that accidentally hurt or angered someone we care about?

How can we know if an offense is unintentional and if a person is still a safe person with whom to be in relationship? Since unintentional offenses aren't meant to deliberately harm a person or a relationship, when someone learns they've offended us, a safe person responds with genuine remorse, not pride.

SUMMING IT ALL UP

Not all conflict is created equal. Some relationship issues are big; some are small. Wise people discern the difference between big things and small things so they know when to address a matter and when to overlook a matter. Conflicts are generally the result of irritations, insults, or issues. When we place our conflicts in the correct box, we'll have better outcomes in finding resolutions. Finally, relational clashes can be intentional or unintentional, and they can be a result of real or surface issues. Wisdom helps us ask questions like "Did this person mean to hurt me?" and "What's the *real* issue here?"

We'll experience more peace and less regret if we identify our conflict correctly—learning to differentiate between intentional and unintentional offenses, surface issues and real issues, and big things and small things.

Lord, help me discern the difference between small things and big things. Help me stop making small things big. God, also give me the courage to stop making big things small. Teach me the difference between righteous anger over real wrongs and unrighteous anger over perceived wrongs. Reveal to me my petty preferences. Give me Your wisdom to overlook annoyances and irritations, and the strength to work through issues by keeping the problem the problem rather than making the person the problem. Help me look out not only for my interests but for the interests of others. Forgive me for words I've spoken that have insulted my family, friends, coworkers, and fellow Christians. Help me realize this is more about me than them. Don't let me rest until I seek their forgiveness and make things right. And God, thank You for forgiving me and giving me newfound tools to handle conflict in ways I won't later regret, amen.

PUTTING PEACE INTO PRACTICE

1. Do you tend to make small things big or big things small? Can you identify an issue you need to release or one you need to address?
2. Is there an irritation you need to overlook? If yes, what?
3. Is there an insult you need to apologize for? If yes, when?
4. Is there an issue you should try to resolve? If yes, how?
5. Consider a current conflict you're facing. How can you focus on the problem and not make the other person the problem? Brainstorm a few ideas.
6. Consider the same conflict (the one you just named). Then

make a list of the other person's possible interests, motivations, values, and desired outcomes. As you formulate how to approach this person, write out how you will take their interests into account. (For example, if you know a person values being respected, you might say something like "I respect your leadership and will support whatever decision you make, but would you mind if I offered a few pieces of information that might help you as you formulate your decision?")

SEVEN

IF EVERYONE WOULD ONLY LISTEN TO ME (OR HOW TO MAKE MISUNDERSTANDINGS A THING OF THE PAST)

Think about your biggest relationship struggle of late. Picture the scenario in your mind until the conflict is crystal clear.

The thought probably puts a knot in your stomach, doesn't it? Your heart may feel heavy. Your jaw may be clenched.

What if you could discover a way to loosen that knot and lighten that load? Sounds like a little slice of heaven, doesn't it?

Lean close because I want to whisper something you need to hear: *You can.*

LEAD WITH LISTENING

Ask one hundred people the best way to deal with conflict, and ninety-nine will likely answer something to do with what to say in the middle of a conflict. While what we say and how we say it are vital to handling conflict successfully, another piece of the conflict picture works like the corner piece of a puzzle. Once this piece is in place, everything around it fits more easily.

The corner piece to conflict is listening.

Most of our day-in, day-out conflicts can be summed up in one word: *misunderstanding*. If 90 percent of our misunderstandings could suddenly disappear, we'd all experience more peace and fewer problems. Listening is the bridge that closes the chasm between misunderstanding and understanding.

However, listening is a lot like driving; everyone thinks they're good at it, but not many actually are.

This turns out to be a much greater contributor to relational conflict than most of us realize. In fact, it's no exaggeration to say the key to more relational peace and less relational regret is to lead with listening.

Maybe you're thinking, *I do listen! The problem isn't that I don't listen to others. The problem is that others don't listen to me!*

But what if the way to get people to listen to *us* is by listening to *them*?

I know, I know, it sounds crazy. But stay with me.

Consider your own relationships—the ones you wish were closer or had less conflict, the ones marked by misunderstandings or defined by disagreements. How often would you say you genuinely listen in those relationships?

Probably less often than you think.

A recent survey found that 96 percent of people rated themselves as good listeners. The article continued: "However, one study showed that we retain only around half of what people say to us. And that's directly after they say it."[1]

Interestingly, it's not that we don't know listening is important; our problem is we're unaware of how little we *actually* listen.

Maybe we overestimate how good we are at listening because we equate hearing with listening. The two, however, are not the same. We hear words, but we listen to discern the *meaning* of the words.

How often have you had the following exchange?

"You're not listening to me."

"Yes, I am. I can tell you every word you just said."

"Yeah, but you're not *listening* to me."

You don't need to be a relationship expert to predict what happens after an exchange like this: conflict. That's because at the crux of most misunderstandings is a lack of listening.

Since listening is a prerequisite for conflict resolution, we must be able to identify when we're listening and—this is key—when we're not. Which, as you will see, isn't as obvious as you might think (thus the misunderstandings people everywhere have *all the time*).

It's obvious that if one person does all the talking, that person hasn't listened to the other person. But if we think listening is merely letting another person talk, we're swimming in the kiddie pool of relational health and peace. Real listening goes much deeper.

Hearing is not listening, though it's part of it. We hear with our ears, but we listen with our minds, our eyes, and our hearts. Since listening requires total engagement, it's nearly impossible to listen with our eyes glued to a cell phone, laptop, or TV. Nor can we listen when we're formulating what we want to say while someone else is still talking.

Listening equals understanding. (Sidenote: understanding doesn't necessarily mean agreement. More on that later.) We have not *actually* listened unless we *accurately* receive the message the other person intended.

IF I THINK YOU SAID SOMETHING YOU DIDN'T SAY, I DIDN'T LISTEN. IF I THINK YOU MEANT SOMETHING YOU DIDN'T MEAN, I HAVEN'T LISTENED.

If I think you said something you didn't say, I didn't listen.

If I think you meant something you didn't mean, I haven't listened.

Most of our day-to-day conflicts can be summed up in one word: *misunderstanding*. But herein lies the problem: listening to understand can be a challenge. Consider the following reasons a group of women gave for why listening can be tough:

- I don't have time.
- I interrupt.
- Honestly, I want the other person to listen to me first.
- I know the outcome; it's always the same.
- I get distracted.
- I already know what they're going to say.
- I get defensive.
- I think, *For heaven's sake! Just get to the point!*
- I lose interest.
- I think about what I'm going to say before they're finished talking.
- I'm tempted to look at my cell phone.

Listening isn't quite as easy as some might think, but its impact has the potential to make our conflicts fewer and our relationships better. Like, *really* better. Here are three reasons why listening really works.

#1: LISTENING LESSENS CONFLICT

Have you ever dreaded a hard conversation? Did you worry the conversation would create more chaos rather than less chaos? Did you wonder, *How do I even begin?*

A few years ago, a friend and I planned to meet for lunch. We chose a restaurant halfway between us, which was still a forty-minute drive. About five minutes before I reached the restaurant, I received a text: "Oops! Probably should have texted you earlier, but my husband invited me to lunch today and I'm meeting him instead."

I took one look at the text and rolled my eyes. *Probably should have texted me earlier? Really?*

I turned my car around to make the forty-minute drive back home and tried to convince myself it was silly to be offended: *She just forgot to tell me about her change of plans. It was a careless mistake.* Minutes later, though, I wrestled with feelings of anger: *How could she be so inconsiderate?* Then five minutes later: *Let it go. She's a friend.* My thoughts and feelings changed so fast I had emotional whiplash!

This was not the first time something like this had happened with this friend. Had that been the case, I would have chalked it up to a simple oversight. But since this was a repeated behavior, I knew I'd create space for bitterness to develop if I ignored the situation. I was also keenly aware that how I chose to handle my frustration had the potential to change our relationship. I wanted that change to be for the better, though honestly, I feared the worst.

I needed to talk to her, but I wondered, *How do I have a conversation where I feel heard but she doesn't feel defensive?*

And isn't that just the relational question of the century?!

I let a day pass before I set an appointment for us to FaceTime. The morning of our scheduled conversation, my heart felt heavy and my mouth felt dry. Finally, the moment arrived. Her face appeared on the screen, and I prayed a silent prayer for wisdom.

I planned to lead the conversation by expressing my feelings, but when I took a closer look at her face, something made me pause. I decided to lead with listening instead.

"Hey! So good to see you! I wanted to chat with you about our lunch. What happened that day?"

"Oh my gosh. I haven't seen you in a while and I was planning on filling you in on all the details when we got together. You see . . ."

My friend went on to explain the backstory while I listened. Prior to our conversation, I'd already formed my perspective and had concocted a "story" surrounding the incident in my mind. (Remember, we discussed our tendency to predetermine narratives in a prior chapter.) But was the story I told myself true? Did I have full understanding?

Not until I listened. Her explanation gave me a complete picture of the circumstance, which helped me formulate what I said next.

"Wow. I had no idea all this was going on in your life. Now your last-minute cancellation makes more sense. Honestly, though, I felt frustrated and dismissed because you waited so late to tell me. I wished you'd called or texted earlier, or at least called me afterward to explain. Can you understand why?"

"Yes, and I'm so sorry. Truthfully, I felt embarrassed because my text was last-minute and I kind of thought it would be easier not to say anything. Thank you for talking to me about this right away so it didn't end up hurting our friendship, Donna. I really appreciate you reaching out."

You could have knocked me over with a feather. I absolutely couldn't have imagined the conversation playing out like it did.

But maybe I should have.

James 1:19–20 says, "My dear brothers and sisters, take note of this: Everyone should be quick to listen, slow to speak and slow to become angry, because human anger does not produce the righteousness that God desires."

When the Bible tells us to "take note," God is effectively saying, "Don't skip over this. Pause and think about what I'm about to say next because it has major ramifications for your life."

So God has our attention now. What, exactly, are we to take note of?

Everyone (that includes you and me) should be (1) quick to listen, (2) slow to speak, and (3) slow to become angry. Why does God give us these instructions? Because (and this is key!) human anger does not produce the righteousness (right internal or external outcomes) God desires.

God gives us a biblical/relational math equation:

QUICK TO LISTEN + SLOW TO SPEAK = SLOW TO ANGER

The opposite is equally true:

SLOW TO LISTEN + QUICK TO SPEAK = QUICK TO ANGER

I'm convinced that my conversation with my friend didn't further the conflict because I paused to listen before I started to speak. Since defenses were defused, she listened to me, too, which enabled both of us to be honest. We ended the conversation feeling connected and content, knowing no hurt feelings stood between us.

No sum of money on earth could buy this kind of peace.

How, exactly, do we start a conversation where we want to lead with listening? We can begin with questions like these:

"What happened?"

"What's your thought on the issue?"

"How do you see it?"

"Tell me your perspective on . . ."

These questions open the door for us to listen and gain a clearer picture of the conflict at hand.

Does being quick to listen and slow to speak always make our relationship issues turn out right? No, but it greatly increases the odds that they will! And, even if things don't pan out as we'd like, we can be certain we've honored God in how we handled relational hard stuff.

#2: LISTENING LIGHTENS INTENSE EMOTIONS

Leading with listening is how God instructs us to handle *our* hurt, anger, or frustration, but how do we handle *another person's* frustration, disappointment, or anger?

Same way: leading with listening.

Several years ago, our normally upbeat daughter found herself dealing with a circumstance that left her frustrated and disappointed. A verbal processor to the core, she shared her feelings with one of her friends. Apparently the conversation didn't go as planned. She expected sympathy, but instead she got truth. "Welcome to real life" were the exact words, I think. Not exactly the warm, understanding response she had hoped for, given her raw emotions.

"I wish you'd been here earlier, Mom. Talking to you always makes me feel better. You listen." It was a very good mom moment.

But hear me on this: *I wasn't always a good listener.* Listening is something I had to learn, often out of desperation because nothing else seemed to work. I'd frequently create *more* drama because I had yet to learn to lead with listening.

Frankly, I didn't understand how to handle other people's difficult, negative emotions. I'd want to do one of these:

- Fix them ("Well, you need to . . .")
- Redirect them ("Look on the bright side.")
- Minimize them ("It's not that bad. You don't really feel that way.")
- Shame them (*Gasp!* "Jesus wouldn't want us to have that attitude!")
- Stop them ("Oh, for heaven's sake, get over it!")
- Ignore them ("I'm busy. I need to be doing other things right now.")
- Dismiss them ("I just can't deal with this!")
- Excuse them ("She's in the terrible twos." "You know how teenagers are." "She's always been this way.")
- Advise them ("You should . . . If I were you . . .")

While most of these strategies have their place, *leading* with any of these eventually results in more frustration and conflict rather than less.

When a person expresses emotion but doesn't feel like they're being understood (read: listened to), they respond in one of two ways:

1. They escalate the conversation.
2. They end the conversation.

It works like this: Your child (husband, friend, or neighbor) feels angry, disappointed, or frustrated. These negative feelings manifest themselves in negative behaviors, attitudes, or words. Any way you slice it, negativity is just plain difficult to deal with, which is why we try to squelch it. Like, now. (Or even better, yesterday.)

Consider this conversation between a mom and her child during the car ride home after school:

> **Child:** "I'm never going to school again!"
>
> **Mom:** "What do you mean you're never going to school? That's ridiculous. You have to go to school."
>
> **Child:** "No, I'm not. I hate school."
>
> **Mom:** "You do not hate school. Don't be so dramatic."
>
> **Child:** "I hate school and I hate my stupid teacher."
>
> **Mom:** "Don't say *stupid*. And don't say *hate*. Jesus doesn't want us to hate."
>
> **Child:** "Well, I do hate her. And I'm never, *ever* going back. You can't make me."
>
> **Mom:** "Oh, yes I can! Now stop with the attitude or you'll be grounded. Do you understand me, mister?"
>
> **Child:** "Forget it. You never understand anyway."

The child crosses his arms and looks out the window, and the minute they get home, he stomps up the stairs and slams his bedroom door for effect. Mom is frazzled, her child is frustrated, and the relationship between mother and son is frayed.

How did a simple drive home from school go so wrong?

Here's what we need to know: if we follow our natural inclination and try to block someone's emotions before we allow that person to express them (because, really, who wants to deal with a surly child, teenager, or spouse?), the other person escalates the negative behavior, and we end up in a power struggle. Things get ugly. If you don't believe me, think back to a time when you expressed frustration to your spouse, friend, or sibling and instead of simply listening to understand you, they tried to fix you or dismiss you.

Didn't go over so well, did it?

People escalate because they're screaming to be understood. The more we fail to understand, the more they escalate. Subconsciously they think, *If I yell louder, cry harder, look madder, or use the silent treatment longer, surely the other person will see why I'm frustrated, angry, or hurt. Maybe then they will seek to understand me.*

If we continue to fail to listen and understand, eventually they'll say something like "You just don't get it! You don't care!" Or, worse yet, they'll clam up, which is code for "This conversation is over, and nothing—and I mean *nothing*—will get me to open up about the situation now." People end conversations when they're convinced they won't be understood. In some relationships, the silent treatment can last for days. Worse, some relationships can end permanently.

Escalate or end.

Doesn't sound very hopeful, does it?

So what do we do? How do we handle difficult, negative emotions when, honestly, we'd really like them to disappear, thank you very much?

First, let me be clear. We can't permit people's negative emotions to run rampant, taking down a whole family, company, church, or community with their continual drama. Nor can we let a toddler's or teen's temper tantrums take the happiness and health of a family hostage. We can't tolerate verbal or physical abuse. We stop these toxic behaviors in their tracks. No exceptions.

That being said, we can handle day-to-day relationship drama by first addressing the internal issue—what's going on in the heart—before addressing the external issue—the resulting words or behavior. We do this by listening with empathy.

Let's go back to our mother-son carpool conversation and add empathic listening to the mix.

Child: "I'm never going to school again!"

Mom: "Wow, honey. What happened today?"

Child: "That stupid teacher gave me a D."

Mom: "I'm so sorry you got a D. No wonder you're upset. What grade did you think you would get?"

Child: "I don't know. I studied really hard and thought I did good on the test."

Mom: "Oh, honey, it's disappointing to expect one thing and get another, isn't it? Is there some way I can help you do better next time?"

Child: "I don't know. Probably nothing. [Short pause.] Maybe you could quiz me?"

Mom: "Great idea! I'd love to help any way I can. And sweetheart, let's not call the teacher stupid, okay?"

Child: "Okay."

When we lead with empathetic listening cues ("What happened? What were your expectations? I'm so sorry. That's disappointing."), it diminishes drama so people can process disappointment without defeat. Further, listening helps us discover the underlying issues. When the mom from the above scenario listened, she uncovered her child's real source of frustration and was able to be a source of help. In the first scenario—the one where Mom failed to listen—the child likely felt controlled. But in the second scenario, the child likely felt cared for.

We shout or shut down when we feel controlled. We share and open up when we feel cared for.

If we resist the temptation to fix an emotion before the other person has expressed the emotion, the conversation is less likely to escalate wildly or end badly. Everyone wins.

One word of wisdom (and I share this as a fellow journeyer who's gotten it wrong more often than I care to admit!): the single biggest factor in our inability to continue to listen with empathy is our propensity to get "hooked" and make the issue a reflection on us.

WE SHOUT OR SHUT DOWN WHEN WE FEEL CONTROLLED. WE SHARE AND OPEN UP WHEN WE FEEL CARED FOR.

For instance, in the second example, the mom led with a question—"Wow, honey. What happened today?"—which invited her son to share further information. But let's suppose she got triggered when her son told her he got a D on his test, and rather than listening, she started lecturing.

"What do you mean you got a D? Didn't you study? I told you playing too many video games would affect your schoolwork. You're grounded!"

When we suddenly erupt, it signals that an issue has hit close to home—which means, for us, the issue has become personal. When conflict becomes personal, it's no longer about you or us. Now it's about me.

In this scenario, the mom may have interpreted her son's grade as a personal failure. She might be thinking, *I'm a bad mom. I should have been more on top of his homework. He'll never get into college with such grades, and it will be all my fault.* In fact, the real issue at stake is helping her child learn to successfully navigate schoolwork, failure, proper preparation, and disappointment.

An eruption is almost always an interruption to the resolution and peace our souls long for.

#3: LISTENING TO OTHERS OPENS THE DOOR FOR OTHERS TO LISTEN TO US

I know what you're probably thinking right about now because it's what I'd be thinking: *But I need to correct my child's behavior. I need to tell my spouse what I wish he'd done differently. I need to tell my sister she's wrong.*

I need people to listen to me!

Yes, you do.

But listen first.

Because if you listen to them, they're much more likely to listen to you.

Eventually.

And isn't that the point?

A friend once confided that she struggled with talking to her teenager about some less-than-ideal choices he was making. So far her efforts had created a war zone in her home. Then one day she paused long enough to take an honest look at her interactions with her son and realized she rarely listened. Sure, she had her reasons; she juggled a full-time job and three kids, her son's schedule was jammed with activities, and she was talkative while he was quiet. Still, my friend knew that if she wanted her son to listen to her advice without becoming angry or defensive, her best shot involved becoming a better listener. This wasn't easy given the fact that he was a teenage boy—not exactly a prime candidate for one-on-one chats.

Despite the obstacles, my friend made a concerted effort to listen whenever her son spoke. She asked questions—not the pressing kind that could close him off, but the "I'm genuinely interested" kind that would open him up. Over a period of several weeks, she noticed a subtle, positive shift in their relationship. They laughed more and argued less. On the day she had a heart-to-heart conversation about some of his choices, it was tense—but not nearly as tense as it would have been if she hadn't paved the way with listening.

A few weeks after their fateful conversation, she learned her son had heeded her advice.

Listening makes others feel valued. A person who feels valued senses they're being cared for rather than controlled, so defensiveness is defused. Therefore, listening allows us to share truth, our perspective, and godly wisdom in ways others will receive rather than reject, ignore, or dismiss. When we lead with listening, we open the door to say, "I'd like to share my thoughts on this issue," and we greatly increase the odds of another person listening to us in the same way we've listened to them.

HOW TO LISTEN

In an article published in *Harvard Business Review*, researchers examined qualities of good listeners. Some findings were expected; listeners set the scene for good listening by removing "distractions like phones and laptops, focusing attention on the other person and making appropriate eye contact." They also work to "understand the substance" of the person speaking: "They capture ideas, ask questions, and restate issues to confirm that their understanding is correct." Finally, the listener "observes nonverbal cues," including gestures, facial expressions, and other types of body language.

Other findings, though, were surprising. These unexpected discoveries separated the good listeners from the great listeners. Most people assume the best listeners listen in complete silence, with only a few "mm-hmms" to encourage the talker. As it turns out, that's not always the case. A great listener "increasingly understands the other person's emotions and feelings about the topic at hand, and identifies and acknowledges them. The listener empathizes with and validates those feelings in a supportive, nonjudgmental way." Sometimes good listeners ask questions that help to clarify, but they "never highjack the conversation so that they or their issues become the subject of the discussion."[2]

In other words, great listeners seek to understand more than they seek to be understood. Some helpful tools and phrases to improve listening include the following:

1. **Ask Open-Ended Questions:** "What's your perspective?" "What happened?" "What are your thoughts?" "What do you think about _____?"
2. **Rephrase What You Heard in Your Own Words:** "So, if I understand correctly, you're saying _____. Is that right?"
3. **Empathize or Validate Emotion:** "I'm sorry you felt disrespected. That's a horrible way to feel."
4. **Allow for Small Spaces of Silence:** People often need a moment to process what they want to say and how they want to say it. Don't jump in to fill the silence too quickly. Silence is often a gateway for others to share more.

You'll want to personalize these phrases to suit your personality and your circumstances, of course. One note of caution: don't use these phrases in some phony "therapist voice" (unless you want to make matters worse, not better!). These tools aren't to be exploited for manipulation, and there's no room to be condescending here either. No one wants to feel like they've been played or used.

Our goal is understanding so everyone involved can experience more peace. Put simply: we diminish the likelihood of misunderstanding when we listen for understanding.

Lord, I confess I'm not always a great listener. I've often sought to be understood more than I've sought to understand. I've tried to get other people to listen to me while being less concerned about listening to them. At times I've been too distracted to listen. At times I've been unwise and made things worse rather than better, simply because I didn't listen. Lord, teach me to listen, for in doing so, You teach me to lead well and love well, amen.

PUTTING PEACE INTO PRACTICE

1. Think of a relationship you'd like to improve, especially if it is currently full of tension. How do you think listening might lessen the tension and improve the relationship?

2. How do you typically handle other people's negative emotions?

3. What prevents you from being a better listener?

4. How have you seen conversations escalate or end in the absence of empathetic listening? How do you think leading with listening could prevent difficult conversations from escalating or ending?

5. Think of a relationship in which you would like to impart your values to someone else. How do you think listening to them could open the door for them to listen to you? Write down one practical way you will be intentional about listening this week.

EIGHT

CONFLICT SHOULDN'T BE A TEAM SPORT

As Holly buckles the kids in the car, her chest tightens. Another holiday means more scrutiny from her mother-in-law. *What will she criticize this time?* Holly wonders. *My parenting? My wardrobe? My work? And why does Joe not see it? Men can be so clueless! Any woman within ten miles would pick up on the disapproving looks, the sarcastic remarks, and the snide, subtle digs.*

After a long drive, Holly, Joe, and the kids arrive, unload the car, and get settled into Holly's in-laws' home.

"My goodness. You bought the kids enough Christmas presents to fill a toy store! I'm sure Joe told you our family got three gifts each, since that's how many Jesus received," Holly's mother-in-law remarks.

Holly does her best to hold her tongue, but her blood starts to boil. *Is she saying I spoil my kids?* Holly's sure of it.

Holly walks on eggshells for the next few days. She tries to avoid hot topics and lets the snarky comments slide. Three days into their visit, though, she's had enough. In their private bedroom, Holly hisses to her husband, "It's either her or me. I'm taking the kids and going home."

Joe feels torn between two women he loves, but he makes up an excuse to his folks about one of the kids not feeling well. Then he loads the car, and he, Holly, and the kids head home. Joe's folks wave goodbye from the front porch, then walk into the house confused and hurt. Joe's mom cries all day.

Meanwhile, Holly and Joe fight all the way home. So much for a merry Christmas.

———— ○ ————

"Emily and Chad McElroy left the church."

"What? Why? They were key leaders in the family ministry."

"Well, I heard from the Davenports that they felt unappreciated for all their hard work. And apparently, Pastor Jim completely ignored them one Sunday. Walked right by and didn't even say hello. Can you imagine?"

"Are you sure? That doesn't sound like Jim."

"Well, the McElroys told the Davenports, and Marcus Davenport is a deacon, so I'm pretty sure he would have said something to Pastor Jim. Pastor Jim *had* to know. But Pastor Jim didn't even apologize! If that's the way they treat people around here, I wonder if maybe I should leave too."

"Did the McElroys ever talk to Pastor Jim directly?"

"Well, you know how it is. I'm sure they just didn't feel they could."

———— ○ ————

Megan picks up her phone and checks her messages. Jen hasn't returned her text. Again.

Megan's thoughts start to spiral. *What's up with Jen? Why am I always the one to reach out? Why do I even bother anymore? Wait— did I do something wrong? Something she didn't tell me about? I don't think so. But then again, maybe. No, I definitely didn't do anything wrong. The problem is her. Why is she like this? I should just forget her. But she's so much fun when she does respond, and besides, we've been friends forever. How would I even begin to cut her out of my life now? But still, maybe I should just ignore her like she's ignoring me . . .*

———o———

What do all three of these scenarios have in common?

Unaddressed offenses.

We now know conflict doesn't magically resolve itself without some form of healthy communication. But frankly, many of us act like if we ignore it long enough, put up with it bravely enough, or vent about it to enough people, the person we're in conflict with will change. Or we hope the hurt, anger, and offense will disappear like a rabbit in a magician's hat.

Unaddressed conflict never disappears, but it does act like a rabbit: It multiplies. Fast.

Have you ever paused to ask why so many of us don't simply address conflict in a healthy way the moment an offense occurs? I'm going to repeat something I said in chapter 2: *The reason so many people feel like conflict is bad is because most of us haven't learned to deal with conflict in a way that makes it turn out good.*

In this chapter we'll dive deeper into what we can say and do to make conflict turn out good. (Let the chorus of hallelujahs begin!)

To start, let's look at a core faulty assumption that can undermine our attempts at healthy conflict resolution. According to the researchers who wrote *Crucial Conversations: Tools for Talking When Stakes Are High*, many of us have bought the lie that says we have to make a choice between two bad alternatives: speak up and risk losing the relationship *or* remain silent and keep the relationship:

> The mistake most of us make in our crucial conversations is we believe that we have to choose between telling the truth and keeping a friend. We begin believing in the Fool's Choice from an early age. For instance, we learned that when Grandma served an enormous wedge of her Brussel-Sprouts Pie à la mode then asks, "Do you like it?"—she *really* meant: "Do you like *me*?" When we answered honestly and saw the look of hurt and horror on her face—we made a decision that affected the rest of our lives: "From this day forward, I will be alert for moments when I must choose between candor and kindness." . . . And from that day forward, we find plenty of those moments—with bosses, colleagues, loved ones, and line cutters. And the consequences can be disastrous.[1]

The researchers also state the obvious, which is that you can only handle conflicts in one of three ways:

1. Avoid them entirely
2. Address them and handle them poorly
3. Address them and handle them well[2]

Of course, none of us looks at the list and says, "Yep, option one will fix the problem," or "Hmm . . . right now, standing in the kitchen with my disgruntled teenager, I think I'll choose option two and handle this poorly." But in real life, most of us pick option one or two more than we care to admit. This is why conflict makes us crazy.

So how do we face conflicts and handle them well? That's the million-dollar question.

THE MILLION-DOLLAR ANSWER

Actually, Jesus was surprisingly clear about how to handle conflict in a way that increases the likelihood for the best possible outcome: "If your brother or sister sins, go and point out their fault, just between the two of you. If they listen to you, you have won them over" (Matthew 18:15).

Some translations include the words "if your brother or sister sins *against you*." Jesus was talking about sin in general, but also relational sins we commit against one another. In the context, Jesus referred to relationships between believers, but the conflict principles Jesus taught transcend religious belief.

Here is the progression of conflict resolution Jesus laid out for His followers:

1. **Step One:** Go Privately
2. **Step Two:** Discuss the Real Issue (Point Out Their Fault)
3. **Step Three:** Note How They Listen
4. **Step Four:** Accept Restoration or Adjust Next Steps

Let's explore each step and see why each one sets us up for the best possible outcome.

STEP ONE: GO PRIVATELY

One big reason we fail to navigate conflict successfully is our propensity to talk *about* others rather than *to* others. Peace is only possible when we stop talking about people and start talking to people, which is why Jesus told us to "go privately."

ONE BIG REASON WE FAIL TO NAVIGATE CONFLICT SUCCESSFULLY IS OUR PROPENSITY TO TALK *ABOUT* OTHERS RATHER THAN *TO* OTHERS.

Functionally, step one is really two steps: go, and go privately. Why make this distinction? Because it's at this first point—the "go"—where most of us get tripped up. If you've ever said any of the following, you've stopped short of Jesus' instructions to "go":

- "I just didn't feel like I could say anything."
- "I don't know when I could say something."
- "They wouldn't have listened anyway."
- "Do you know what could happen if I say something?"
- "I've tried saying something before and it never helps."
- "Maybe someone else will say something."
- "I'll say something to so-and-so, and hopefully they'll say something about the problem."
- "Why do I have to say something anyway? Shouldn't they just *know*?"

In all likelihood, you've made one of these statements, if not all of them. If so, you've bought into this fallacy: *I can speak up or I can keep the relationship, but I can't do both.*

But what if Jesus told us we *can* do both? What if Jesus told us *how*?

Because this is *exactly* what Jesus taught us.

Most people fall somewhere on what I call "the conflict continuum." On one extreme you'll find the avoiders; on the other extreme you'll find the attackers. But the sweet spot in the middle—the people who are positioned for the best possible outcome—are the addressers. These are the folks who handle conflict the way Jesus intended.

THE CONFLICT CONTINUUM
←——Avoiders ——Addressers —— Attackers——→

Some people avoid hard conversations to keep the peace. And while this may sound good (noble even), in reality, avoiding—like attacking—is a selfish response. Both avoiding and attacking focus on what's best for me: *I don't want to feel uncomfortable*; *I don't want to deal with difficulty*; *I don't want to compromise.* Addressing tough topics focuses on what's best for the relationship. This is real love.

Recently, my daughter, Ashton, told me about her prayer to invite God into hard conversations. "God, don't let this be a conversation between two; let this be a conversation between three."

Our hardest conversations can become our holiest moments for God to do works of reconciliation, clear up misunderstandings, and repair past hurt. But for a holy outcome we must follow Jesus' instructions: "If another believer sins against you, go privately and point out the offense" (Matthew 18:15 NLT).

Honest conversation, the kind where we address rather than avoid or attack, is a prerequisite for healthy conflict resolution. Let that sink in for a minute. Snide comments, sarcastic remarks, yelling, disapproving facial expressions, silent treatments, changing the subject, dropping hints, gossip, slander, and criticism never result in lasting change, real reconciliation, or relational peace.

Plus—and I'm just going to be blunt here—these behaviors are sinful. If we choose these actions instead of going to the person who sinned against us, we add our sin to their sin. Then their behavior is not the only problem; our behavior becomes a problem too. No wonder conflict gets ugly.

So why do we use these ineffective tactics instead of having the conversation that could clear the air, reconcile a relationship, and bring us the peace we long for?

Fear and familiarity.

Fear focuses on what could go wrong; familiarity focuses on what we've always done. Neither promises peace. If we allow fear or familiarity to drive our response to conflict, we use backdoor methods to manipulate others to change. In doing so, we see others as objects to be controlled, obstacles to be removed, or opposition to be defeated rather than people we are connected to and care for.

Jesus told His followers to walk through the front door by engaging in honest dialogue. Open, honest conversation is front-door communication. No hidden agendas. No passive-aggressive ploys.

The "go" instruction presupposes that we'll talk face-to-face or voice-to-voice. Of course, when Jesus spoke about handling sin and offenses, texting and emails weren't invented. Though these things make our twenty-first-century lives easier, they also make our efforts at conflict resolution harder. One of my communications professors said that in a face-to-face conversation, 90 percent of all communication is nonverbal, which includes things like facial expressions, tone of voice, and body language. Only 7 percent of communication is verbal, meaning the actual words we speak. Given the enormous influence nonverbal cues play in our ability to decipher what people mean when they speak, is it any wonder our attempts to resolve a conflict over text or email often fail? Person-to-person is the way to connect. Conflict is already hard. Why make it harder?

Which is why Jesus said that if someone sins against you, *go to them.*

But Jesus also told us to go privately. "Just between the two of you" are His exact words.

If only Christians obeyed this command.

Think about it: if we handled conflict the way Jesus instructed, addressing issues one-on-one rather than involving others unnecessarily, there would be much less gossip, slander, hateful social media fury, online bullying, or ghosting. We would also see less bitterness, divorce, and relational devastation, as well as fewer church splits and family fractures. The unity Jesus prayed His children would experience would actually have a shot at becoming reality.

Plus, when we address an issue privately, we avoid embarrassing another person, which in turn decreases the odds of defensiveness and increases the odds of receptivity. In addition, people say things online or over text that they would *never* say to someone's face. Looking a person in the eye has a way of restraining our reactions.

If you are married or are a parent, make a commitment to never correct your child or spouse within earshot of others. All of us should resolve never to rebuke or correct someone via social media either. Private conversation communicates respect. Respect is the soft soil out of which conflict resolution and healthy relationships grow.

STEP TWO: DISCUSS THE REAL ISSUE (POINT OUT THEIR FAULT)

At this point half of you are thinking, *Finally! It's about time I get to tell the other person how they're wrong!* The other half are thinking, *Oh, no. I thought going to the person was the hard part. How am I ever going to talk about what's honestly bugging me?*

Fear not. Let's see what Jesus meant when He said to "point out their fault."

First, the word translated as "point out" is the Greek word *elégxō*, which means "to convince with solid, compelling evidence."[3] And no, Jesus wasn't giving us permission to be the judge and jury. Instead, Jesus told us to use concrete examples of the offending behavior. Sometimes this is harder than it seems. What we *think* is clearly wrong behavior might, in fact, be a misunderstanding or a misperception on our part.

In a previous chapter we discussed how we tell ourselves a story in the middle of every conflict. These stories attribute motive to actions. Unfortunately, instead of starting with "once upon a time," our conflict stories begin with thoughts like *He did such and such because* _____. *She said that since* _____. Our stories of what happened and why usually paint us in the best possible light, and they paint the other person in the worst possible light. Perhaps this is one reason most of our conflicts end up more like nightmares than fairy tales.

Here are a few examples of how this plays out:

- She is late because she doesn't value my time; I was late because I got caught in traffic.
- He spoke abruptly because he's insensitive; I spoke abruptly because I was rushed.
- She took over the meeting because she's domineering and doesn't trust me; I took over the meeting because the conversation was getting off topic.
- They got annoyed because they're entitled; we got annoyed because we're concerned.

Alternately, our story may color us in shades of black and the other person in shades of white. This happens when we concoct stories to excuse another person's bad behavior rather than address it. For example: "He screamed at me because I deserved it. All teenagers get angry at their parents. That's why he swears at me."

The stories we tell ourselves so we "understand" often lead to more misunderstanding, not less.

With this in mind, let's revisit the second example at the beginning of the chapter. Remember when Pastor Jim walked by the McElroys without speaking? Remember how it offended them? But what if Pastor Jim didn't see them? What if Pastor Jim was preoccupied with a crisis phone call he'd just received, and his mind was elsewhere? (Sidenote: this scenario happened to someone I know.) Would this knowledge change how the McElroys felt about their pastor and their church? Probably.

We need to be open to the possibility that what we see as concrete evidence might be less concrete slab and more memory-foam mattress.

> WE NEED TO BE OPEN TO THE POSSIBILITY THAT WHAT WE SEE AS CONCRETE EVIDENCE MIGHT BE LESS CONCRETE SLAB AND MORE MEMORY-FOAM MATTRESS.

At this point you might be wondering, *But how can I figure out what actually happened so I know I have concrete evidence?* We lead by listening (remember the last chapter?), and we open the door for listening by asking questions *before* making assumption or comments.

But let's also consider the alternate scenario. Suppose Pastor Jim *did* overlook the McElroys. And suppose he consistently failed to express appreciation to the folks who volunteered week after week, year after year, which left the McElroys wondering if they should leave the church. How might the outcome have been different if, at the first sign of discontent, instead of talking *about* their pastor to others, the McElroys met with Pastor Jim and respectfully spoke *to* Pastor Jim in the hopes that everyone in the church would feel valued, appreciated, and excited about their service?

Should I Always Go to the Other Person?

Now let's consider two aspects of "going": whether to go and when to go. If going to the person who offended you sounds impossible, you're likely thinking: *But you don't know my pastor, spouse, co-worker, or mother!*

You're right. I don't.

Good outcomes are not guaranteed, even when we go to the person who sinned against us, because good relationships require two humble people (remember chapter 4?). Additionally, in some extreme cases (such as when abuse has occurred), going to the person is not the wisest option. And, as we discussed in chapter 5, some minor issues are better left overlooked. In most instances, however, we have zero chance of seeing relationship improvement if we don't talk about the pressing issues.

Of course, *how* we broach a sensitive subject is vital too. Galatians 6:1 reminds us, "Brothers and sisters, if someone is caught in a sin, you who live by the Spirit should restore that person gently. But watch yourselves, or you also may be tempted."

Tone of voice, timing, an attitude of humility, and genuine concern for the other person must undergird any effort to point out a fault. If our timing or tone of voice is off, the conversation will likely be too. We can't be brash and then blame the other person when they bristle over our attempt to point out their fault.

How we say what we say is as important as *what* we say.

When Should I Go?

Jesus, in His infinite wisdom, told us to go privately and point out the fault. Implied is a sense of urgency. We don't wait until we can't take it one more minute to address a sin or offense—which, incidentally, is what most of us do. (Come on. You know it's true.) This rarely goes well.

The beauty of attending to identifiable behaviors sooner rather than later is twofold. First, it allows us to respectfully address one issue at a time, which is less threatening, less overwhelming, and less likely to be refuted. Second, it prevents us from enduring the pressure and pain caused when we let offenses build over time.

But, like everything relational, wisdom and timing are always key.

Let's return to Holly's Christmas situation. Could Holly be *certain* her mother-in-law meant to criticize her parenting? Maybe. Even so, should Holly point out her mother-in-law's fault on the spot? Not necessarily. Sometimes a wiser first course of action is to redirect critical comments by taking charge of where the conversation goes next. Jesus was the master of this.

What if, when her mother-in-law made the comment about the number of Christmas gifts she'd purchased for her kids, Holly had said something like "Joe told me about your three-gift tradition. What a wonderful way to honor Jesus and teach your kids the real meaning of Christmas! Did Joe ever mention my mom went a little crazy at Christmas? My best childhood memories are of my Christmas experience, mainly because it was the only time we got a lot, and it made the holiday special. I hope to combine both Joe's and my family traditions for our kids. I'm doing my best to make Christmas fun *and* Christ-centered like you did."

In all likelihood, this positive redirection will end the critique.

But if not (and sometimes it doesn't), a more forthcoming approach will be necessary.

For instance, in the third example at the beginning of the chapter, direct conversation will be necessary for Megan to successfully navigate her situation with her friend Jen, who fails to reply to her texts. But before we get to Megan and how she should go about that conversation, let's get a fuller picture of what Jesus meant when He said to "point out their fault." Each word is rich with meaning and practical for us as we approach another person about a fault.

> **Point Out:** We can't be general or vague when conflict resolution is at stake. People can't change "in general," and they won't know why we're making such a big deal out of something if we're vague. In addition, we must be sure we discuss the real issue, not a peripheral one. Sometimes people who feel uncomfortable with conflict talk around the real problem rather than addressing the problem head-on. They'll drop hints like little bread crumbs, hoping they will lead the other person to the realization of what the problem truly is. Or they'll address a group hoping the one person who's the source of conflict will clue in. The result is confusion rather than clarity. Neither party ends up feeling like the conversation resolved the conflict.
>
> **Their:** "Their" describes the other person's action. This presumes we've already done the work of taking the log out of our own eye, we've committed to being humble, and we've examined any part we might have played in the conflict. If we haven't examined our part, we start there before pointing out someone else's part. But after we've examined our motives and any part we played in the conflict, we point

out their offense *respectfully*, without beating around the bush. People who address issues rather than avoid issues or attack people shoot for 100 percent honesty and 100 percent respect.

Fault: "Fault" is singular, not plural. This means we discuss one issue at a time, not twenty issues that happened over time. We can't back up a dump truck full of grievances and unload them on our spouse, child, or coworker all at once. If we do, the other person will feel defensive and overwhelmed. Meanwhile the real issues—the ones that can be fixed right now—will get buried beneath the rubble.

Okay, so now that we're clear, let's get back to Megan and her friend to examine how a direct, open, and honest conversation can take place.

Megan might say something like "Jen, I hope you know how much I value our friendship. Though we've been friends for years, I've noticed the last several times I've texted you to get together, you don't return my texts until days later. At first I chalked it up to us both being busy—I know that can happen. I get it. But I sent texts twice last week, and three times the week before. This feels disrespectful, and honestly, it hurts my feelings. I'd rather hear an honest answer from you than hear nothing at all."

When we open a dialogue by validating the person or our relationship with the person (saying, "I value our friendship," "I want both of us to experience a good working relationship," or "I care about you"), pointing out a fault is easier for us and less painful for the other person. Plus, this assures that our motive is restoration rather than being "right."

Notice also how Megan gives Jen the benefit of the doubt ("I chalked it up to us both being busy"), but she is specific in her comment ("I sent texts twice last week, and three times the week before"). Megan also acknowledges her feelings ("this feels disrespectful") and speaks candidly about how she would like their relationship to move forward ("I'd rather hear an honest answer from you than hear nothing at all").

Then Megan listens for the response.

What Jen says next will tell Megan everything she needs to know about how to proceed. In fact, Jesus gave us the heads-up on what to look for at the end of Matthew 18:15, with step number three.

STEP THREE: NOTE HOW THEY LISTEN

In Matthew 18:15, Jesus tackled offenses that rise from actual sin, not just perceived offenses. This is not a case of what I think versus what you think.

So, for the sake of simplicity, let's say we have a legitimate, airtight complaint. Our brother or sister *has* sinned against us, and to the best of our ability, we've taken Jesus at His word and handled the situation like He instructed us: We've examined ourselves and our own motives. We've allowed for the possibility that the story we've told ourselves about the situation might not be the full picture. We've been honest about any part we played, even inadvertently. We've talked to the person privately. We've led by listening. We've moved forward by being both respectful and honest in our communication. We've provided a specific example of an offense. What next?

Spoiler alert: it's an *if*, not a *when*.

When implies an automatic outcome. *When* would lead us to expect that if we follow Jesus' way, humble ourselves, and speak with both grace and truth, others will too. But real life tells us this isn't always the case.

Don't you love that Jesus allows for this contingency with one simple word—*if*? *If* they listen, not *when* they listen.

Not all conflict can be adequately resolved the first time we broach an offense. Not all people will agree with our assessment of the situation. Not all people will admit their sin. Not everyone is willing to listen and respond. But—and this is crucial—no conflict can be resolved unless we try. Some people *will* listen. Some *will* apologize. Some *will* make things right.

Let's go back to Megan and Jen's conversation. After Jen learns her actions have been disrespectful and hurt Megan's feelings, she responds with "Oh, Megan. I am so sorry! I have been busy, but that's no excuse for ignoring your texts. Your time is as valuable as mine, and your friendship is important to me too. I'm sorry, and now that I know, I'll try to respond immediately, or at least as soon as I possibly can."

But what if Jen doesn't listen? What if Jen gets defensive? What if she blames Megan? What if she brushes off Megan's concern by calling her too sensitive?

Jesus taught us how to handle that too. Sometimes other godly people need to get involved; other times we need to recognize a relationship isn't healthy and move on.

We'll dive more deeply into this type of situation in a later chapter. For now, let's consider the possibility of a wonderful outcome.

STEP FOUR: ACCEPT RESTORATION OR ADJUST NEXT STEPS

The best-case scenario, of course, is conflict resolution and relationship restoration. This must be our goal. The endgame is not being "right" but redeeming a relationship whenever possible.

Several years after my "I want to burn down the church" debacle, JP received a handwritten card from one of the elders at our former church—a place that hurt us so deeply. The portion I remember most vividly went something like this.

"At the time, I didn't fully understand all the ways we (the elder board) handled things wrongly, though you and others tried to tell us. I guess we got caught in a self-justifying spiral of behavior. Frankly, we were led by fear rather than faith. Until recently, I didn't grasp how deeply our actions hurt you and your family.

"I am so sorry. We were wrong. *I* was wrong . . ."

When I read the card, I was speechless. Words can't adequately express the healing that took place that day.

Would we have liked to receive this note seven years earlier, in the midst of the conflict, heartache, and drama? Of course. But the words "at the time, I didn't fully understand" shed light on why reconciliation wasn't possible then. Sometimes spiritual and emotional growth must take place before we can fully see the impact of our behavior on others, or theirs on us. Growth takes time.

It bears noting that even years after the offense, reconciliation was possible because the offender had the integrity, humility, and conviction of heart to acknowledge his part in the offense. He could have easily rationalized away an apology, saying, "After this long, an apology won't matter. Why bring up the past?" Or "Since I was part of a group, I don't need to take individual responsibility." Wisely, though, he realized that where relationships are concerned, it's rarely too late to make right a wrong.

When we seek to handle conflict God's way—going privately and gently, addressing the real issue with respect, and listening for the other person's response—sometimes restoration happens immediately. Sometimes restoration never happens, and sometimes, in a mysterious way only the Holy Spirit can orchestrate, it comes later than we'd like. But it comes.

Wherever, whenever, or however restoration comes, it's nothing short of beautiful.

When Jesus told us how to handle an offense, He offered us the best possibility for the relational peace we long for. Let's take it.

Lord, I confess I haven't always handled conflict according to Your Word. I've talked about others rather than talked to others. I've avoided or attacked when I should have addressed. I've been insensitive or too sensitive. I've been vague, hoping others would guess what bothers me. I assumed things I shouldn't have and failed to handle conflict in ways I should have. But God, You are teaching me new ways of relating— thank You! Jesus, thank You for the instructions You gave so I could have more peace and Your children could experience more unity. Now that I know what to do, help me do it, amen.

PUTTING PEACE INTO PRACTICE

1. When it comes to conflict, are you more of an avoider or an attacker? Which would those closest to you say you are?
2. Consider a current conflict. Have you talked *about* the other person or *to* the other person? How has your choice affected your personal peace and your relational peace?
3. Have you told yourself a story about another person (*they did _____ because they _____*) before having *all* the facts?
4. Do you tend to discuss one offense at a time, or do you store up offenses over time? How do you think addressing one offense at a time would increase your chance of resolving conflict and increasing peace?

5. Reread Jesus' instructions: "If your brother or sister sins, go and point out their fault, just between the two of you. If they listen to you, you have won them over" (Matthew 18:15). Write down one way you will obey Christ in a current conflict.

NINE

DO WE REALLY HAVE TO
DO THIS? NOW?

My friend greeted me with four words: "It's been three days."

I was confused. "Three days since what?"

"Three days since my husband and I have spoken to one another."

If her husband had been across the world fighting a war, three days of silence might not have been a big deal—but the only war being fought in my neighbor's world was between two people who shared a bed. And, although there were no raised voices or slammed doors, the lack of peace she felt was profound. Their disagreement might as well have been loud enough to reach from her house to mine.

RESTORING PEACE

You've probably heard this biblical mandate: "Do not let the sun go down on your anger" (Ephesians 4:26 ESV). But what does this mean, exactly? What happens if we don't resolve conflicts quickly? Is it really a big deal? And if it is a big deal, how do we handle conflicts in a way that makes the relationship better, not worse?

These are the questions on the table in this chapter.

Actually, my friend's conflict with her husband wasn't wrong. Conflict isn't wrong; conflict is inevitable. Nothing is necessarily wrong with us, or with our relationship, if we *experience* conflict.

Before you move on from the previous sentence, pause for a moment. Think about the conflict you have going on right now—the one with the spouse, child, coworker, or friend. No doubt the conflict generates all kinds of negative emotions—ones you'd like to end right now—but the conflict itself doesn't mean your relationship is bad or irreparable, or that the person you're in conflict with is bad or unforgivable. This is an important truth to grasp because millions of us believe conflict *is* bad. Intellectually we know it's not, but emotionally we function like it is. Somewhere along the way, through our family of origin or religious circles, or maybe through our traumatic experiences, we embraced the idea that conflict, by definition, is bad.

As a result of this faulty belief, we avoid conflict. We deny conflict. We demonize conflict and the people who cause it. We leave relationships because of conflict. The implications of how we view conflict are staggering.

Though nothing is necessarily wrong with us or our relationships if we experience conflict, *something is wrong if we don't resolve conflict well.* I've said it before, but I'll say it again: what makes conflict good or bad is not its presence but our practices during its presence.

This should give you hope. We can't avoid conflict altogether, but we can learn healthy practices in the midst of conflict!

In my Bible, Ephesians 4:17 and following is preceded by this heading: "Instructions for Christian Living." The passage contains a boatload of relationship guidance, but before the passage tackles the nitty-gritty practices for working through conflict successfully, the apostle Paul warns us to avoid handling conflict the way the world (or our flesh) dictates: "So I tell you this, and insist on it in the Lord, that you must no longer live as the Gentiles [unbelievers] do, in the futility of their thinking. They are darkened in their understanding" (Ephesians 4:17–18).

WHAT MAKES CONFLICT GOOD OR BAD IS NOT ITS PRESENCE BUT OUR PRACTICES DURING ITS PRESENCE.

What does this mean, exactly? And how does it play out in our real-life conflicts?

A few months ago, I overheard a conversation in the locker room at my gym. A few thirtysomething gals gathered on a bench, lacing up their tennis shoes. One needed relationship advice.

"My boyfriend didn't do what I asked him to do yesterday. How do you think I should handle it?"

"Drop him," said the first gal.

"Next time he asks you to do something, don't do it to get back at him. He needs a taste of his own medicine," said another.

"Give him the silent treatment. That'll teach him," said a third.

These were *actual* comments from *real* women on how to deal with conflict. Was any of it wise? Or helpful? Would any of this advice resolve the conflict, solve the problem, and increase the chance of real change or lasting peace?

No. No. Definitely no.

The point is obvious: not all relationship advice is good advice. And, more important, there should be a difference between the way a Christian handles conflict and the way a nice atheist handles conflict.

In Ephesians 4:17–18, God tells us not to handle our relationships like the unbelieving world. Their thinking is futile, and they are blinded in their understanding. Each word here is jam-packed with meaning pertinent to *you* and *your* relationships. In fact, understanding these two verses can save you *years* of relational heartache.

The Greek word that's translated *futility* in this verse carries a few connotations, including "ineffective."[1] So the verse could be rendered, "I tell you this: You must no longer live as the unbelievers do, in the ineffectiveness of their thinking."

Do you want to make ineffective, futile choices in how you handle relationship conflict? Of course not! Neither do I. This is why Paul insists we think differently than we once did. Our family of origin might have taught us ineffective ways of resolving conflict, our girlfriends might give us futile advice, and reality TV may model harmful examples—but guess what? We don't have to live this way any longer. We have a choice!

Essentially, we handle conflicts based on one of two factors: instinct or insight. Unhelpful methods of managing conflict are based on instinct: Does it *feel good* in the moment? Helpful methods, on the other hand, are based on insight: Will it *produce good* in the long haul?

How do we know if we're operating on instinct rather than insight?

Instinct doesn't consider outcomes. Instinct operates on habit and emotion.

Instinct says:

You hurt me; I'll hurt you.
You yelled at me; I'll yell at you.
You ignored me; I'll ignore you.
You gossiped about me; I'll gossip about you.
If I can't get my way, I'll show you!

Or, if your personality is bent in a different direction, instinct might not take the form of fight but flight or freeze. Avoidance, emotional shutdown, silent treatments, passive-aggressive behavior, and appeasement are all instinctual responses too.

Can you see why relating based on instinct is a train that never gets off the misery track? One of the greatest misconceptions of our time is "If it feels right, it is right."

God's instructions for healthy relationships continue in verse 18: The unbelievers "are darkened in their understanding." The word translated "understanding" is the Greek word *dianoia*, which is similar to our English word *diameter*. Stay with me here because this is key—and you're going to love it!

Diameter is the distance from one side of a circle to another. The Greek word *dianoia* (understanding) is defined as "movement from one side (of an issue) to the other to reach *balanced*-conclusions; full-orbed reasoning . . . that literally reaches 'across to the other side' (of a matter)."[2]

Translation: Wise, godly choices—the kind that enhance my chances of resolving conflict, experiencing healthy relationships, and living in peace—consider how what I do today affects the quality of my relationship tomorrow. Wisdom thinks things all the way through.

Here are some examples of thinking ahead with my choices:

- **The way I communicate with my spouse today will shape the connection we experience tomorrow.** Therefore, I will communicate kindly and clearly today, because my choice to communicate better now affects my chance of closer connection in the future.
- **The extent to which I listen to my toddler today will determine the extent to which my teenager talks**

to me tomorrow. **Therefore, I will put down my cell phone and listen. My choice to focus on my child today improves my chance of her being open with me later.**

- **The dedication I give to my friends today will affect how devoted we are to one another tomorrow.** Therefore, I will stop waiting for my friend to text me. I will text her first because the choice to reach out will improve my chance of maintaining her friendship from now on.
- **The way I handle conflict with a coworker today will influence how congenial we are tomorrow.** Therefore, I will talk to my coworker today about our issue. The choice to work it out will help our chance of being on good terms for weeks to come.

Can you see how the choice to handle relational hiccups based on insight rather than instinct greatly increases our chance of peace? We cannot divorce the relational choices we sow today from the relational consequences we reap in the future. To believe otherwise is to be darkened in our understanding and futile in our thinking. This is why Paul tells us—insists, actually—that we *not* live this way.

No one has good relationships by chance. Good relationships are forged by choices.

SO WHAT CHOICES DO I NEED TO MAKE?

Paul began Ephesians 4 with an appeal. And, like all good teachers, he explained what a life worthy of our calling as followers of Jesus looks like: "As a prisoner for the Lord, then, I urge you to live a life worthy of the calling you have received. Be completely humble and gentle; be patient, bearing with one another in love. Make every effort to keep the unity of the Spirit through the bond of peace" (Ephesians 4:1–3).

We're to make *every* effort (not just *some* effort) toward peace. In earlier chapters we discussed the importance of humility and gentleness as qualities for conflict resolution, but I find it interesting that these qualities aren't just essential to handling conflict; according to Paul, they are essential to living a life worthy of being called a Christian!

Then, in verse 25, Paul got über-practical as it relates to conflict and the choices we must make in the midst of it: "Therefore each of you must put off falsehood and speak truthfully to your neighbor, for we are all members of one body. 'In your anger do not sin': Do not let the sun go down while you are still angry, and do not give the devil a foothold" (Ephesians 4:25–27).

CHOICE #1: PUT OFF FALSEHOOD

"Put off falsehood" is a fancy way of saying, "Don't be dishonest—not even a little bit."

This turns out to be much harder than it sounds. A few weeks ago, I was cleaning out a drawer and stumbled across a funny note someone gave me years ago called "Nine Words Women Use." I have no idea where this originated, and researching the reference led me to believe it's been passed around in email chains and social media posts for years. But it made me laugh, and it illustrates how often we fail to put off falsehood when faced with conflict.

NINE WORDS WOMEN USE

1. **Fine:** This is the word women use to end an argument

when they are right. You need to stop talking and realize she's done.

2. **Five Minutes:** If she is getting dressed, this means half an hour. If you pressure her to be ready in five minutes, she'll take forty, and a fight will ensue. Instead, realize "five minutes" means you can relax and watch the ball game.

3. **Nothing:** This is the calm before the storm. *Nothing* means "something," and you should be on your toes. Arguments that begin with "nothing" usually end in "fine."

4. **Go Ahead:** This is a dare, not permission. Don't do it!

5. **Loud Sigh:** This is a nonverbal statement often mistaken by men. A loud sigh means she thinks you're an idiot and wonders why you're wasting her time standing here arguing about nothing. (Refer back to #3 for the meaning of *nothing*.)

6. **That's Okay:** This means she wants to think long and hard before deciding how and when you will pay for your mistake.

7. **Thanks:** If a woman thanks you, do not question or faint. Just say, "You're welcome." However, if she says, "Thanks a lot," she is using pure sarcasm and she is not thanking you at all. *Do not* say, "You're welcome." That will bring on a "whatever."

8. **Whatever:** This is a woman's way of saying, "You're sleeping on the couch tonight, buddy."

9. **Don't Worry About It; I've Got It:** Another dangerous statement meaning, "I asked you to do something several times, but now I'm doing it myself." This will likely result in a man asking, "What's wrong?" For the woman's response, refer to #3.

All kidding aside, honesty is the foundation upon which all healthy relationships are built. Remove honesty and replace it with lies, half-truths, innuendos, or speculations, and the relationship will crumble.

Personally, I love how the phrase "put off falsehood" provides a visual image of what to do during conflict. Picture yourself seated at a table. On the tabletop lie all the possible things you could say or think when you're upset: things you'd love to say but probably shouldn't; things you don't want to say but probably should; motives you suspect are true but aren't unquestionably accurate. Now picture yourself picking up each thing, one by one, and examining it carefully. Then, if it's not truthful, picture yourself laying it down.

So, choice #1: Put off falsehood.

CHOICE #2: SPEAK TRUTHFULLY

The flip side of the "don't lie" coin is "speak the truth." The word *truth* here refers to facts or reality as opposed to speculation. Again, this concept is harder than it seems. If you've ever had an exchange that went something like this, you know this to be true:

"Where do you want to go for dinner?"
"I don't care. Anywhere is fine."
"Okay, let's try that new Chinese place."
"Chinese? Really? Hmm . . . I don't really feel like eating
    Chinese."
"Okay, where would you like to go?"
"Anywhere is fine."

See what I mean? Many of us have a difficult time even speaking the truth when it comes to what we want for dinner! How much more, then, do we struggle with speaking the truth in complicated, tension-filled situations? Even worse, sometimes we presume to "know the truth" about others when, in fact, we don't.

And yet, without speaking the truth, there can be no resolution—and without resolution, we live with constant tension and a lack of peace. We hope our family and friends will figure out what we want, why we're hurt, or why we're upset; but when they don't, we end up with more hurt and anger, which means a blowup is just around the corner. We blame their lack of sensitivity when the burden of responsibility falls squarely on our shoulders; we didn't speak truthfully but instead hoped they'd guess accurately.

TRUTH IS THE MESSAGE, BUT LOVE MUST BE THE MOTIVE AND THE MEANS BY WHICH THE MESSAGE IS COMMUNICATED.

How we speak the truth is crucial too. The Bible tells us to speak truth in love. Put another way, truth is the message, but love must be the motive and the means by which the message is communicated.

If either component—truth or love—is missing or lacking, a conflict cannot be resolved well and will likely escalate. More important: if we speak truth without love, or if we communicate love but fail to speak truth, we haven't communicated the way God intended.

We know this.

However, when emotions run high and we're in the heat of the battle, it's difficult to *do* this. It's also true that it's difficult to do this when emotions run high and we'd rather run from the battle.

Years ago, I served on a committee with a woman who could best be described as domineering. Her take-charge personality had merit, for sure, but it was also off-putting. As a result, every member of the committee resigned, leaving only her and me to handle all the details of a large event.

Someone has to say something, I thought. *She needs to know she's driven everyone away.* Since I'd been versed in what the Bible says about "going to your sister and pointing out her fault" and I was certain what I would say was true, I decided to confront her.

But not before I told a friend about my plan.

My friend looked me square in the eye and used her most matter-of-fact voice: "You are not going to say anything."

"What? Why not?" I protested. "She needs to know!"

My friend pressed. "What's your motive?"

"How can she grow if she doesn't know?"

My friend didn't buy it. "Yeah, I know that sounds super spiritual and all, but what's your *real* motive? Because I'm pretty sure this isn't about her growth; it's about your frustration."

Ouch. Bull's-eye.

I was itching to speak the truth, but my motive wasn't love or even the desire for a better working relationship. My real motive—and I'm just going to be honest here—was something more along the lines of "Stop being yourself—because everything about you makes my life more difficult and is driving me insane." If I'd ventured to "speak truth" out of personal aggravation rather than genuine concern, the relationship would have been damaged, and I would have lived to regret it. This isn't to say I should have never had a truthful conversation with my fellow committee member—simply that my motive needed to be right before doing so.

You can go to the bank on this truth: big personal emotions can lead to big relational messes. This is why both our motives and our methods must be right. Intense feelings should come with a warning sign: "Proceed with caution."

I've seen some people use the guise of "speaking truth" when the underlying motive was to shame or manipulate. On social media some self-proclaimed "truth tellers" post scathing rebukes or quips that only serve to hurt or discourage others. Actions like these *create* conflict and are in direct violation of Christ's command to "do to others as you would have them do to you" (Luke 6:31).

It's deceptively easy to convince ourselves that being "right" justifies what we say or how we say it. We dress up motives in spiritual-sounding language with phrases like "I'm just speaking truth," "God told me to tell you," or "If you were really walking with the Lord, you'd see this the way I see it." We can even quote Scripture (but only the parts that back up our viewpoint).

Where speaking the truth is concerned, attacking is never the answer. But neither is avoidance. Truth without love is not biblical truth, just as love without truth is not biblical love.

One of the easiest ways to simultaneously clarify our motive and give us the confidence necessary to speak the truth in love is to ask one simple question: *In what specific way will my comment help the person and help our relationship?*

CHOICE #3: DON'T LET THE SUN GO DOWN ON YOUR ANGER

God's Word presupposes that we *will* get angry. Anger is not sin. Anger is an emotion. How we handle the emotion of anger determines whether it's sinful or sanctified.

What the Bible says next shows us the key to *how* to be angry and yet not sin (which, in my estimation, is the million-dollar question). Are you ready for the answer? Here it is:

"Do not let the sun go down while you are still angry" (Ephesians 4:26).

The word *let* implies a choice. I can allow a conflict to fester by replaying what they said, what I said, what I wish I'd said, why they said what they said, why I said what I said, why I am right, why they are wrong—on and on like a never-ending merry-go-round. Handling conflict this way is no joyride; it's an emotional roller coaster that makes us sick with bitterness, anger, and resentment.

Or I can choose to be brave, follow God's instructions, and resolve conflict before it has a chance to steal my peace and kill my relationships. Not letting the sun go down on our anger means following Jesus' mandate to go privately to our brother or sister (which we explored in the previous chapter) in a timely manner—the same day if possible. Always sooner rather than later.

But you might be thinking, *Is it really a big deal if I don't address a conflict quickly? Can't it wait?*

The health of a relationship is *directly* linked to the amount of lag time between an issue and when that issue is addressed. The shorter the lag time, the better the relationship. So the question is *Do I want this relationship to be healthy?* If the answer is yes, relational concerns must be tended to as soon as possible.

Frankly, though, many of us don't *want* to work through conflicts quickly. We're hurt. We're afraid. We're unpracticed at addressing conflicts rather than avoiding them, so the idea of openly talking about relationship issues makes us uncomfortable. We'd rather drop hints and hope the other person figures out why we're upset. Or we'd rather play nice and keep the peace, even when we know, deep down, this won't bring peace. *At. All.* We give in and, in doing so, give up something of ourselves. As a result, our relationship leaves us empty rather than full. Stressed rather than serene.

Let me offer a word picture that illustrates why conflict resolution is essential for a relationship to thrive.

Envision conflict as a brick. Each conflict we have with another person is a brick laid down between us and them.

One brick may not seem like a big deal—a small thing, really. However, when we fail to resolve a conflict and instead revisit the infraction in our mind, it has the same effect as repeatedly stubbing our toe on the brick. *Ouch!* Common sense would dictate that we remove the brick; we know if we don't, we'll keep stumbling over it.

But here's where this gets real: many of us leave the brick where it is. We might even think, *I know I should address this problem*, but we don't. We're too angry. We're too tired. The risk is too high. We don't know how to proceed. We assume the other person will never change, and this whole thing is their fault anyway. The list of excuses is endless.

Instead, we go to bed, get up in the morning, and life moves on. We go to work, take the kids to school, run to the grocery store, make dinner. We forget about the conflict, at least while we're occupied. Suddenly, though, another conflict happens, and now we're faced with a choice: deal with it or dodge it. We decide to dodge it, and in doing so, we lay down another brick.

Before long, we are building an entire wall. Satan starts helping us out. He even hands us the bricks.

As you read the following verses, pay special attention to the word *and*: "'In your anger do not sin': Do not let the sun go down while you are still angry, and do not give the devil a foothold" (Ephesians 4:26–27).

When we fail to resolve conflicts, we give the devil a foothold in our life and our relationships.

Stop. Go back. Read that last sentence again. Unresolved conflict is an open door for the devil to destroy you and the relationship you are in right now—the one filled with conflict that torments your heart, soul, and mind.

Think of it like this: You hear a knock at your door, so you open it. But you soon realize the person at your door isn't a friend; he's an intruder bent on robbing you of everything you hold dear. You try to shut the door. However, the intruder has placed his foot in the threshold of the door. His foot prevents you from fully shutting him out, though you try and try. The intruder now has a hold on your most private sacred space—your home.

Giving the devil a "foothold" means opening the door for the Enemy to steal our relational harmony, our testimony, our family, our friendships, and our unity. He plunders our peace in the sacred space of our hearts and minds.

When we let the sun go down on our anger, we open the door for the Enemy to walk into our life and rob us blind. Returning to the previous mental picture, it means accepting another brick from his hand—one fashioned out of bitterness or resentment. Remember, the verse reads, "Do not let the sun go down while *you* are still angry" (emphasis added). Anger is primarily a personal issue before it's a relational issue.

I want to pause right here and say something I don't want you to miss: *What we do with our bricks determines what happens in our relationships.*

Over time, unresolved conflict becomes one brick laid upon another brick, laid upon another brick. Soon, a wall is formed. Soon, two people who were once in relationship can no longer see each other. All they can see is the wall of problems.

There's no hope, they think. *The issues between us are too monumental.*

How did the wall get there?

One brick—one unresolved conflict—at a time.

Too many of us live with walls. They're killing us and our

relationships, leaving devastation in their wake. This, friend, is why God says, "Do not let the sun go down while you are still angry, and do not give the devil a foothold."

One word of caution: some people like to talk through issues right away, while other people need time to think before they speak. If we pressure people who require space to talk sooner than they're ready, they'll feel attacked. If we (indefinitely) put off people who need to talk, they'll feel like we're avoiding them. In either case, conflict will escalate, another brick will be laid down, and the wall will grow.

So now what? Some of you are reading this and thinking: *This. Is. Me. I've built a wall.*

First, don't hang your head in defeat. You're reading this right now because God is equipping you.

Next, remember that a wall is removed the same way it was built—one brick at a time. From this point on, choose God's way: work through issues, talk about problems, listen to another's perspective. Put what you're learning into practice.

But be forewarned: the wall won't likely come down in a day, just as it wasn't built in a day. However, over time, each time you face a conflict instead of allowing it to fester, a brick will be removed. Sight can be restored. Hope can be found. And, maybe best of all, peace will become possible.

What's the takeaway? Make a choice to resolve a conflict when it's still a single conflict, and you'll never erect a wall.

Lord, I don't want walls; I want relational peace! Thank You for showing me choices I can make to find this peace: laying aside falsehoods, speaking the truth, and resolving conflicts one at a time. I commit myself to following Your instructions.

Help me make wise decisions in the middle of my present life conflict so I can avoid future life regret, amen.

PUTTING PEACE INTO PRACTICE

1. In this chapter, I said, "We cannot divorce the relational choices we sow today from the relational consequences we reap in the future." Make a list of all the possible ways you could handle one conflict you repeatedly face. Cross off any words or behaviors that will lead to negative consequences in the future. Look at the possible positive choices that remain on your list. Prayerfully consider which option would be best in your circumstance.

2. Have you ever failed to "put aside falsehood" or "speak the truth in love"? Do you need to apologize for anything you've said or done? If you're currently experiencing conflict, write out what you can say that will be both truthful and loving. (If this proves challenging, ask yourself: *How would I want someone to discuss the issue with me?*)

3. How have you allowed the devil to hand you a brick in a relationship?

4. Have you built a wall between yourself and someone else by repeatedly letting the sun go down while you are still angry? (Word to the wise: if the phrase "still angry" resonates with you, you've likely built a wall, even if it's a small one.)

5. What is one way you can begin to dismantle the wall you've built?

TEN

WAYS WE MAKE THINGS WORSE INSTEAD OF BETTER

In the history of human conflict, no one ever calmed down after someone said, "Calm down!"

Have you ever noticed how some words have a way of making conflict worse rather than better? Words have power. Like the tiny knob on your oven, one small shift in word choice can cool emotions down or heat emotions up.

Personally, I'd love someone to figure out what all of those triggers are and share them in a concise list so we don't have to keep saying and doing things that simply won't help.

Since I couldn't find that kind of list, I made one myself.

In this chapter we'll explore some of the most common conflict mistakes, why they don't work, and what to do instead.

You're welcome.

CONFLICT MISTAKE #1: EXAGGERATION

Wife: "Why don't you ever ask what I think? You always do whatever you want to do. You never listen to me."

Husband: "That's not true. You never remember the nice things I do. You're always overdramatic."

Conversations like this one take place in marriage, parenting, business—everywhere. The common conflict communication mistake here is exaggeration. When we use words like *never* or *always*, we've likely overstated the facts. The problem with exaggeration is that words like *never* and *always* can be easily refuted, which takes the conversation off course.

For example: "You never . . ."

"That's not true. Remember that one time I . . ."

Now we're sparring over "that one time" instead of discussing the topic we really wanted to address. Once a conversation is off course, the real issue—the one that generated the conflict—gets overlooked and remains unresolved. And, instead of discussing a legitimate concern, we're splitting hairs over *never* and *always*.

Using exaggerated terms poses a secondary problem: they're usually paired with the word *you*, as in "you never" or "you always." Nothing puts people in a posture of defensiveness faster than the word *you*. When defenses are up, the likelihood of a healthy discussion goes down. As a result, conflict is almost never resolved in a mutually beneficial way.

How can we avoid exaggeration? For starters, ditch the words *always* and *never*. Instead, focus on one or two recent examples of the offense you want to address and begin with "I" statements ("I feel" or "I thought") rather than "you" statements. If possible, before you begin the conversation, have an idea about how to move forward in a constructive way.

CONFLICT MISTAKE #2: WORRYING ABOUT WHO STARTED IT

Ask any parent what their kids say when siblings fight, and "They started it!" will almost certainly top the list. The assumption behind "They started it" is that behavior is justified if someone else instigated the conflict. Every word or deed gets couched behind the excuse "It's not *my* fault."

What's true for kids is true for adults. When we focus on who started a conflict, we're prone to justifying our bad behavior too.

The seemingly simple principle is difficult to practice, though, because we *like* to assign blame. But when we spend the bulk of our time assigning blame (either out loud or in our heads), we place the responsibility of conflict resolution on the person at fault; if you started it, it's up to you to end it. This means, functionally, placing our personal peace at the mercy of another person.

So what do we do in lieu of worrying about who started a conflict? Focus less on who's at fault and focus more on how to move forward.

CONFLICT MISTAKE #3: INSULTS AND NAME-CALLING

"You're such a jerk."

"How can you be so stupid?"

"What an idiot!"

"You're just like your father."

"Stop being such a drama queen."

"You're a loser."

Seeing these insults in black-and-white likely made you cringe. After all, they seem so . . . *mean*.

In fact, they are mean. When we resort to insults and name-calling, we *mean* to be mean. An insult is *intended* to injure. Sure, we may say "I didn't really mean it" afterward, but even heartfelt remorse can't fully remove the sting.

Insults and name-calling diminish the possibility of a positive conflict outcome, and they damage the relationship of the people in the conflict. God is clear about words that tear down: "Don't use foul or abusive language. Let everything you say be good and helpful, so that your words will be an encouragement to those who hear them" (Ephesians 4:29 NLT).

Make a commitment not to insult or name-call—even if someone else does. These behaviors always—and I use that word intentionally—make relational conflict worse, not better.

CONFLICT MISTAKE #4: BEING DISMISSIVE

We are dismissing another person's concern when we say things like this:

"Whatever . . ."

"Stop freaking out."

"Relax!"

"Just get over it."
"Why are you making such a big deal out of this?"
"Again?!"

Or it can happen with our facial expressions and body language:

An eye roll.
A loud sigh.
Shaking our head with a look of disgust (often accompanied
    by crossed arms).
Looking down or looking away.
Feigning interest when it's obvious we've emotionally
    checked out.

The problem with dismissiveness is that it sends a message of disrespect and disregard. Essentially we're saying, "I don't care enough about you to take your concerns seriously." It's a short walk from disrespect and disregard to the destruction of a relationship.

What can we do if we don't feel like hearing someone's complaint?

If we don't want to listen due to time constraints or emotional constraints (for example, we're not emotionally prepared for a conflict at the moment), we can say something like "I know this is important to you, but right now I don't have enough bandwidth to listen well. Can we talk about this when I can give you my full attention?" Then we make it a point to reengage with the person later.

If we're not sure why the problem is a big deal, we can say something

IT'S A SHORT WALK FROM DISRESPECT AND DISREGARD TO THE DESTRUCTION OF A RELATIONSHIP.

like "You sound upset, and I want to really hear you out. Could we go back to the beginning because I think I missed something."[1]

CONFLICT MISTAKE #5: ASSUMING THE WORST

If we find ourselves in conflict with a person who's an otherwise decent human being, this mistake is particularly lethal. People who routinely assume the worst before they have all the facts almost always do so as a defense mechanism born from past hurt. Subconsciously, they think, *If I believe the worst from the start, I won't be blindsided by the worst in the end.*

We make assumptions because we've encountered a similar issue previously. Therefore, we conclude the past is indicative of the present. But when we assume the worst before we gather all the facts, we make ourselves judge and jury before a discussion has even begun!

At this point, this conflict mistake makes relational messes even messier: when we render a predetermined verdict, we back the other person into a corner—leaving them no other choice but to defend themselves from the get-go. Since most people perceive defensiveness as evidence of guilt, our perception that we are correct to assume the worst gets reinforced.

Even if we are wrong.

As a result, truth becomes more difficult to discern. Motives are questioned, which undercuts trust for both parties.

Negative assumptions fracture friendships, mess up marriages, and force our kids to wonder why they should even bother doing the right thing if we're just going to assume they did the wrong thing no matter what.

So what do we do instead?

Believe the best unless we have proof of the worst.

Some may think, *Isn't this naïve? We can't stick our heads in the sand and pretend people don't do wrong!*

No, we can't. However, if we start with the presuppositions that other people are out to intentionally hurt us, can't be trusted, or only look out for themselves, we'll soon find ourselves very lonely indeed. No one wants to be in a relationship with a person who consistently paints them with the brush of negativity.

CONFLICT MISTAKE #6: REACTING TOO QUICKLY

You open your laptop and read an email criticizing something you've done. You glance at your phone and see a nasty text. You open the door of your home and hear bickering in the background.

What do you do?

If you're like most people, you react.

Nine times out of ten, reacting makes conflict worse, not better.

When we react, we're acting out of emotion. This means we'll likely say or do things we'll later regret. Sure, we may feel empowered as we type out our perfectly worded defense to the critical email (in all caps, mind you), but we'll probably feel embarrassed the moment we hit send.

Whenever we feel our chest tightening, our blood boiling, or our jaw clenching, it's a good sign the best response is to wait. There's no law that says we must respond in the moment. Twenty-four hours allows us to sleep on it, pray over it, and, when necessary, get counsel for it. A good night's sleep gives our emotions a chance to settle and our brains a chance to select the best way to respond.

CONFLICT MISTAKE #7: DISPLACED ANGER

Have you ever had a bad day at work then been grumpy with your spouse? Have you ever had an argument with your spouse then lost your cool with your child? Have you ever had a run-in with your teenager then lost it with a stranger?

If you've experienced any of these scenarios, or ones like them, you've experienced displaced anger.

Displaced anger happens when we take out our frustration, anger, or hurt on someone other than the source of these emotions. Family, close friends, or roommates can easily become the targets for displaced anger simply because they are *there*. We can also displace our anger internally when we blame ourselves for something that is factually not our fault. This happens frequently where abuse is present.

Displaced anger makes conflict worse for two major reasons:

1. It prevents us from addressing issues with the correct person or people.
2. It provokes conflict with a person or people with whom we have no real reason to be angry.

How can we avoid misplaced anger? When we feel angry, frustrated, upset, agitated, or hurt, ask two questions:

1. Why do I feel this?
2. Who is involved in the scenario that generated this feeling?

But what if *you* become the target of someone else's displaced anger?

Years ago, I was upset over something that happened in my child's classroom. That evening as I chopped vegetables for dinner, I expressed my anger over the situation while JP sat at our kitchen island listening. Our conversation (ahem . . . my venting session) went smoothly until, out of the blue, I stopped chopping, turned to JP, and said something like "You know, if you would have acted differently, this might not have happened." My anger at my child's classroom situation morphed into anger at my spouse.

Wisely, JP looked at me with complete calm. "Donna, it's okay that you're angry. And I'm happy to listen to your venting. But don't make this about me. It's not about me. It's about what happened at school."

I dropped my guard—and the kitchen knife I'd been wielding—and got quiet. He was right. He was *right*.

Sometimes it may be necessary to speak the truth in love by saying, "I'm not the real object of your anger, so please don't take your anger out on me."

CONFLICT MISTAKE #8: WRONG PLACE, WRONG TIME

Timing is everything in comedy.

Timing is also everything in conflict.

In the last chapter we discussed the importance of resolving conflicts before bitterness has an opportunity to take root or a wall between two people is built. Ephesians 4:26 tells us not to let the sun go down while we are still angry, but does this mean we must always work through conflict on the spot?

To correctly apply this biblical admonition, it's helpful to consider the preceding phrase: "In your anger do not sin." There are moments when an attempt to resolve an argument in real time will only make things worse, not better. For example, an argument between spouses ten minutes before bedtime, when both parties are exhausted, is unlikely to produce a positive resolution. In fact, trying to talk about an issue when we're tired, hungry, distracted, rushed, or stressed will likely turn "in your anger don't sin" into "in my anger I sinned even more"!

There are times and places where the better part of wisdom is to wait.

There are also times and places we should *never* engage in conflict; to do so will only make things worse. We shouldn't argue in public. We shouldn't argue over email or text messages. We shouldn't argue on social media. We shouldn't argue on our way to church. (Come on. You've done it. So have I—and I'm the pastor's wife!)

In conflict, as in life, there's a time and a place. Choose the time and place wisely, and you'll experience more peace and less regret.

CONFLICT MISTAKE #9: SHOUTING AND THE SILENT TREATMENT

Shouting and the silent treatment are two sides of the same conflict coin.

They're both ineffective methods of communicating the same message: "I want you to know I'm mad, sad, or feeling bad." While one gets louder and aggressive to gain attention, the other gets quieter and passive to gain attention. Both shouting and the silent treatment are power plays for control.

Why don't these tactics work?

For starters, when we yell, we're effectively saying, "Hear what

I want you to hear!" But when we yell, the other person's brain goes into fight, flight, or freeze mode. This means they neurologically *can't* hear, think, or speak in a way that can help resolve the problem.

And neither can we. When we yell in anger, we don't use the thinking (cerebral cortex) part of the brain; we use the emotional (limbic center) part of the brain. We fly off the handle, and our ability to be rational flies out the window. Conflict moves from bad to worse. As Proverbs 15:1 reminds us, "A gentle answer turns away wrath, but a harsh word stirs up anger."

When we employ the silent treatment, we're saying, "See what I want you to see." But when we go silent, we force (or try to force) the other person to figure out why we're upset without the benefit of knowing our perspective. In effect, we're asking people to read our minds. Which, of course, is impossible.

What does this mean for real life? Because of how our brains are wired, shouting and the silent treatment have exactly zero chance of being effective in changing behavior and resolving conflict in lasting, positive ways. Yes, these methods may get attention in the short term (that's why so many of us use them), but in the long term, they do more harm than good.

So what can you do if you're prone to shouting to get your point across?

First, the only person you should ever tell to "calm down" is yourself. A little self-talk when you're tempted to yell (or even when you're already in the middle of a rant) can go a long way to settle the atmosphere (and your soul).

Then, remember these words: *Say it, don't shout it.*

On the other hand, what can you do if you're prone to using silence to get your point across?

Remember these words: *Speak up, don't clam up.*

When you stop shouting, stop pouting, and simply say what's bothering you, you take the first step in being seen, being heard, and healing your relationships.

CONFLICT MISTAKE #10: BRINGING UP THE PAST

> IF WE BRING UP THE PAST WHEN WE'RE DEALING WITH CONFLICT IN THE PRESENT, WE HINDER THE RELATIONSHIP FROM BECOMING HEALTHIER IN THE FUTURE.

If we bring up the past when we're dealing with conflict in the present, we hinder the relationship from becoming healthier in the future.

So why do we do it?

Bringing up the past indicates unforgiveness at play. When we harbor hurt, we're haunted by another person's behavior. Since we haven't released the wrong, we want to remind them of the wrong. We still hurt and want them to hurt too. The inevitable outcome of bringing up the past is *everyone stays hurt*.

Sometimes we bring up the past to exert control. "Remember what you did last time? I should be in charge this time." "Have you forgotten what happened when you _____? You should listen to me this time instead." Or "You admitted your guilt last time around, so I'm sure you're guilty this time too. I know I'm right."

Other times we bring up someone else's past to avoid responsibility for our behavior in the present. "Well, what I did isn't as bad as what you did when you were my age." Or "You have a lot of nerve talking to me about this given your history."

Unforgiveness. Control. Sidestepping personal responsibility. These behaviors never lead to better relationships.

Bringing up the past is a conflict mistake because it keeps relationships frozen where the focus remains—in the past.

MOVING FROM CONFLICT MISTAKES TO CONFLICT MANAGEMENT

The ability to identify our conflict mistakes is one of the most important steps toward experiencing more peace and less regret in our relationships. After all, you can't fix what you don't know is broken.

As an added benefit, if we avoid conflict mistakes, we can prevent many conflicts from starting in the first place. After all, few of us get into heated battles with people who don't shout or shut us out. We generally get along with others who believe the best about us instead of assuming the worst. We live in harmony with those who listen to rather than dismiss our concerns.

When we know what makes conflict worse, we become free to choose words and actions that make conflict better.

Lord, I don't want to say or do things that make conflict worse. Holy Spirit, convict me before I handle conflict in a way that will harm my relationships. Convict me afterward if I slip into old patterns that prevent me from enjoying the relational peace You want me to have. Help me repent so I can experience more peace and less regret, amen.

PUTTING PEACE INTO PRACTICE

1. Review the top ten conflict mistakes, listed below. Circle any mistake that you repeatedly make. (Be honest. Most of us make some mistakes repeatedly.)

   1) Exaggeration (*always, never,* etc.)
   2) Worrying About Who Started It
   3) Insults or Name-Calling
   4) Being Dismissive
   5) Assuming the Worst
   6) Reacting Too Quickly
   7) Displaced Anger
   8) Wrong Place, Wrong Time
   9) Shouting or the Silent Treatment
   10) Bringing Up the Past

2. Sometimes we make one mistake with one person but a different mistake with another person. For example, we might shout at our kids but use the silent treatment with our spouse; we might react too quickly with a neighbor but dismiss a coworker. Make a list of your recent conflicts. What mistakes did you make in handling the conflict, if any? What can you do differently in the future?

3. Brainstorm ways you can avoid your primary mistake and replace it with a wiser response. Write down a few ideas you'll commit to practicing.

ELEVEN

HOW TO STOP CONFLICT BEFORE IT STARTS

What if you could trade internal angst for internal peace by discovering how to communicate thoughts, feelings, needs, and desires with grace, truth, and zero regret? And, as a result, lessen the chance of conflict? Sounds like a little slice of heaven, doesn't it?

For this to become a reality, we must first deal with our expectations—which is often easier said than done.

During our first year of marriage, JP and I had a nightly ritual:

1. Come home late after a long day's work
2. Put on our pajamas
3. Turn on the TV
4. Eat vanilla ice cream together

This Monday–Thursday routine rarely deviated. (Don't call us if you're looking to shake things up in your life. Just sayin'.)

One summer evening, after a particularly long day, we sat

snuggled on our sofa dressed in our pajamas. After about ten minutes, JP got up and headed for the kitchen. From where I sat, I could hear the cabinet door open, and then the freezer door. I heard the spoon clank against the bowl. I knew exactly what my husband was doing.

So when JP walked into our family room with one bowl of vanilla ice cream, I was surprised.

"Where's *my* bowl of ice cream?" I wondered aloud.

"What do you mean?" JP was genuinely confused.

"We always eat ice cream together. Didn't you know I'd want ice cream too?"

"How could I have known you'd want ice cream unless you told me you wanted ice cream?" JP said innocently. He was sure his logic was airtight.

News flash: conflict is rarely logical.

I shot off the couch, stomped into the kitchen, and jerked open the freezer door, muttering something super encouraging like "I've married the most clueless man on earth" under my breath. To this day I have no idea why a ridiculous episode over ice cream made my blood boil.

But it did.

At this point, JP announced he was going to take out the trash.

"Go right ahead, buddy," I barked as I spooned ice cream into my bowl.

The funny thing was JP had to walk past our open kitchen window to take out the garbage. I watched as he walked past once. Then, on his way back into the house, he stopped in front of the screen and pressed his face up to the open window with a giant smile. *What in the world?* I wondered.

With the same big grin still on his face, JP uttered a single phrase that changed our relationship forever.

"Expectation without communication leads to frustration."

I laughed. Out loud. "Did you just make that up?"

He smiled broadly. "Yep. Just thought of it myself." (Fun fact: This phrase has been repeated on social media, on podcasts, and in blogs. So if you've heard it before, now you know where it originated!)

JP was right. Expectation without communication leads to frustration. So, it follows that if we want to lower the frustration level in our relationships, we must raise the level of our communication.

Instead of assuming JP would "just know" I'd want ice cream, if I'd simply said, "While you're getting yourself ice cream, would you get me some too?" he would've gladly obliged. Then we would've experienced a peaceful evening enjoying a movie and our dessert.

EXPECTATION WITHOUT COMMUNICATION LEADS TO FRUSTRATION.

Conflict averted.

HOW TO MANAGE EXPECTATIONS

What is an expectation, exactly? Here's my homespun definition: an expectation is something we assume *and* desire to happen—something that, if it fails to happen, leads to frustration, anger, or hurt.

Expectations can be minor. (The newlywed gets upset because her husband doesn't take out the trash like her dad always did.) Or expectations can be major. (A parent goes ballistic when her college-age kid gets a DUI.) Expectations can be personal. (A couple feels hurt when they aren't invited to a wedding.) And they can be professional. (An employee who's certain she'll be next up for a promotion gets passed over.)

What makes expectation complicated is the fact that we're often unaware of our expectations until they go unfulfilled. We think things like *Of course he'll take out the trash like my dad did.* Or *He would never drink and drive. He knows better.* Or *I can't imagine we wouldn't be invited. We've known them for years.* Or *I'm positive I'll get the promotion. After all, I'm next in line.*

In my case: *He'll know I want ice cream. We eat it together every night.*

An expectation is the assumption of a certainty. Because an expectation is tied to an assumption, and few things in life are certain, an expectation is a disappointment waiting to happen. An *unexpressed* expectation is a disappointment *destined* to happen.

Some people say the solution to the problem of expectations is not having any. Of course, this would be ideal; it's just not real. Here's a three-step approach to managing expectations in real life: be aware of them, communicate them with clarity and kindness, and keep them realistic.

1. BE AWARE OF EXPECTATIONS

Some expectations are easy to identify. "I expect you to be on time" and "If you tell me you'll do something, I expect you to follow through" are two examples of common expectations most people embrace. Some expectations, however, are more personal and can be a bit harder to pinpoint. We feel upset, disappointed, or angry but can't quite figure out why. When these emotions threaten personal and relational peace, we can pause and ask ourselves, *Do I feel this way because I had an unmet expectation?* The answer to this question will often unearth an unspoken expectation, or an expectation we didn't even know we had!

An awareness of our expectations is vital if we want to lessen conflict and heighten peace. We cannot communicate what we have not identified. Since expectation without communication leads to frustration, if we remain ignorant of a relational expectation, we won't be able to communicate said expectation to others. As a result, we'll live with ongoing frustration, hurt, or anger, but we'll never really get to the root of *why*. The peace we long for will remain out of reach.

2. COMMUNICATE EXPECTATIONS WITH CLARITY AND KINDNESS

Once we become aware of our expectation, we must communicate it. When we communicate an expectation on the front end, we avoid conflict on the back end.

However, clarity is key in communication. Without clarity, confusion reigns. Where there is confusion, there is chaos. Where there is chaos, there is conflict.

Clearly communicating our needs, desires, and expectations is vital to the health of all relationships. For instance, frustration and conflict with our child can be minimized when we clearly communicate an expectation early on, instead of venting frustration later. "Stop being such a slob" can be replaced with "After you finish your snack, remember to put your dishes in the dishwasher."

Instead of flying off the handle when our teen comes home late, we can prep them beforehand: "I want you to have a wonderful time tonight. Remember, curfew is eleven o'clock. That doesn't mean 11:05. I can't wait to hear all about your evening. Have a great time!"

At work we can communicate our expectations by saying things like "Just a friendly reminder: I need the report by two o'clock today." If we're interviewing a potential employee, we can say, "The expectations around here are high. Here's a list of the work demands. Is that an expectation you can meet?"

Naturally, *how* we communicate our expectation is crucial too. Scripture instructs us to speak the truth in love.

Expectations have a way of always being expressed—eventually. If we fail to communicate our expectations up front, we'll inevitably communicate our expectations on the back end with words or actions that are anything but loving.

Whenever expectations are involved, the best advice is this: don't wait to communicate.

Expectation without communication *will* lead to frustration.

It bears noting that the word *expectation* has the potential to trigger a conflict rather than avert a conflict. As we learned in an earlier chapter, the root of conflict is a power struggle. The phrase "I expect" may be perceived as controlling rather than communicative, especially in a peer-to-peer relationship. "I expect you to" has undertones of "do this, or else." It can come across in an off-putting way that gives the other person no option but to comply or create conflict. Unless we're in a position of authority, such as a boss or a parent (or in some marital issues, such as "I expect you to be faithful"), it's best to exchange the phrase "I expect" to "I'd like," "I need," or "I want."

3. KEEP EXPECTATIONS REALISTIC

Two common themes run through each of the previous illustrations. First, the expectations are clear; second, the expectations are realistic.

Expectations must be rooted in reality. For instance, we can sincerely desire a close relationship with our mother, father, or spouse—and we can even communicate our desire clearly and sincerely—but if that person is incapable of genuine connection, our unrealistic expectation will leave us discouraged, defeated, and depressed. We can clearly communicate an expectation that our child should make straights As, but if the child's capability is closer to a B, we'll become demanding or, worse, demeaning when that unreasonable expectation isn't met.

However, when we keep our expectations realistic and communicate them clearly and kindly, we can lessen the potential for conflict. What's more, we trade internal angst for internal peace because we've discovered how to communicate needs and desires with grace, truth, and zero regret.

KNOW HOW TO HANDLE CRAZY IDIOSYNCRASIES

Communicating our expectations is one way to stop conflict before it starts, but there are others.

Shortly after his college graduation, my son, Taylor, came home for a weekend visit. True to Jones-kid form, he sat perched on my kitchen counter while I prepared dinner. (I have no idea why my kids prefer our counter over our chairs while I'm cooking, but they do. And I kind of love it.)

"I have a theory about human relationships," Taylor mentioned casually.

If I'd been distracted by making dinner before, I wasn't now. Taylor had my complete attention.

"Really? I'd love to know what it is."

"Everybody has a little bit of crazy," he said with a laugh, but in all seriousness too.

I nodded in agreement. "You couldn't be more right!" I paused a beat while processing the truth of Taylor's theory. Then Taylor continued.

"The key to avoiding conflicts is to not let *their* little bit of crazy become *your* little bit of crazy."

All human beings (you and me included) have relational idiosyncrasies—triggers that cause us to overreact—which my son affectionately dubbed our "little bit of crazy." This is normal.

Here are a few real-life illustrations:

- Getting lost
- Being late
- Long wait times
- Mindless paperwork
- Overstimulation
- Boredom
- Multitasking
- Disorganization
- Messiness

These circumstances, and ones like them, trigger the worst sides of our personalities. We may get easily irritated, overly frazzled, or weirdly quiet. See? A little bit of crazy.

How we deal with another person's trigger will determine whether the crazy becomes a conflict. Or not.

To deal wisely with relational idiosyncrasies, we must possess these:

1. Sufficient awareness to spot triggers that make us or another person overreact
2. The tools necessary to avoid getting sucked into another person's "little bit of crazy"

A close friend recently admitted that in the early years of her marriage she didn't understand how to deal with triggers. For example, if her husband became frazzled over being lost, she made things worse by saying something like "What's the big deal? We'll figure it out. Calm down." Of course, this did not calm things down. At *all*.

Or she'd get mad that he was mad, which made them both mad multiplied by a thousand.

One day, though, she realized getting lost was her husband's trigger. Without fail, getting lost took him to the edge of crazy town. So the next time he got lost, she gave him space to express his frustration. And you know what? His aggravation passed without a harsh word between them.

Of course, this presupposes the ways we handle things that make us crazy are minor, not major. Raging, throwing things, screaming, or abusing are not little idiosyncrasies; major infractions like these require hard-line boundaries.

However, when we're in relationship with otherwise good-hearted people, the best way to deal with someone's "little bit of crazy" is *don't*.

Now that we know how to deal with other people's idiosyncrasies, how do we deal with our own? Because—and let's just be honest here—sometimes *our* idiosyncrasy is what causes the conflict.

The best way to deal with our trigger isn't to deny it ("I am *not* overreacting!"). It isn't to deflect it ("Well, at least the way I'm handling this isn't as bad as what you would've done"). Nor is it to excuse it ("I'm only acting this way because . . .").

The best way to deal with our trigger is to own it. And let others know you own it too.

Let me give you a personal example. I have three adult kids. I also have an unsatiable "once a mom, always a mom" desire to tell them to be careful. I'm aware that this is part of my "little bit of crazy," which, in turn, has the potential to drive them crazy. So that my crazy doesn't make my kids crazy, I'll sometimes say, "I know what I'm going to say is more for my peace of mind than for your instruction, but please—drive safely."

Even as I type these words, I'm aware that a more mature response would be to deal with my trigger and trust that my kids know to be careful. However, I'm not quite there yet. (Look for instructions on how to eradicate our "little bit of crazy" in my next book.) For now, I'll own my quirks.

When we own our triggers, it helps others too—which lessens the chance of conflict.

WHEN CONFLICT IS UNAVOIDABLE, HAVE A PLAN READY

So far we've explored how to deal with inevitable idiosyncrasies and how to communicate our needs, desires, and expectations in the hopes of stopping conflict before it starts. However, real life tells us that even when we communicate our needs, desires, or expectations clearly, the other person won't always comply. Even when we show grace for other people's triggers, sometimes the overreactions hold us hostage.

Sometimes we can't stop conflict before it takes us captive.

So we need a plan.

Hostage negotiator and former police psychologist George A. Kohlrieser indicates that forming an emotional connection is crucial to his work: "When someone feels you are honestly interested in them, they will be much more willing to connect and bond. Out of that bond, negotiation works." Other hostage negation principles include demonstrating your goodwill and intentions and pausing to take a break when things get tense.[1]

These same three strategies can serve us well too.

1. ESTABLISH AN EMOTIONAL CONNECTION

While our conflicts won't likely be as stressful as the life-or-death situations hostage negotiators encounter, all conflict holds us hostage to some degree. When conflict is present, our peace is held hostage, our emotional and spiritual freedom are held hostage, and our thoughts are held hostage. Sometimes our reputation or our health is held hostage. In instances like these, the same strategies that work for hostage negotiators can work for us.

During a conflict, we can establish an emotional connection with the other person by saying things like this:

- "I can tell this is important to you."
- "I know you feel strongly about this."
- "I'd feel the same way if I were in your shoes."
- "I understand why you're upset."

When used wisely, humor can defuse tension and establish an emotional connection too. It's hard to stay angry when you're laughing.

2. DEMONSTRATE GOOD INTENTIONS

To demonstrate goodwill, we can say things like this:

- "I'd like to help if I can."
- "Let's see if there's a way to resolve this so we both feel satisfied with the outcome."

179

- "I want to do what's best for everyone involved."
- "I'm on your team."

Often, establishing emotional connection and demonstrating good intentions will be enough to de-escalate conflict. Other times it won't. In these instances, pausing to take a break is the best option.

3. PAUSE WHEN THINGS GET HEATED

We are not obligated to become enmeshed in someone else's emotional mess.

A pause is not avoidance. A pause is an opportunity for intense reactions to settle, and taking a break gives both parties the opportunity for an emotional reset. We might say something like "I can see that we're not going to be able to figure this out right now. Let's push pause." Or "I'd like to think about this for a little while. I'll get back to you soon."

WE ARE NOT OBLIGATED TO BECOME ENMESHED IN SOMEONE ELSE'S EMOTIONAL MESS.

When you receive pushback on the pause, a more direct "I'm going to end the conversation now" might be necessary. Other times a more indirect approach to establishing a pause will work best. For instance, we can press pause on an opinionated dinner guest by saying something like this: "That's an interesting perspective. Who'd like coffee? I also have tea. How many for each?" Then make a beeline for the kitchen.

No one has the right to hold us hostage by generating unnecessary conflict.

Real-life hostage situations aren't planned, but—and this is critical—*hostage negotiators have plans for the unplanned.* In other words, they know certain conflicts are bound to happen, so they prepare their response prior to the pressurized moment.

We can do the same. Perhaps we have a critical relative who's joining us for the holidays; in advance, we can practice how we'll respond in case the conversation becomes cutting. We may be in relationship with a person whose moods fluctuate by the hour; we can resolve to stay sweet even if they turn sour. Perhaps we have a friend or family member who consistently asks us to give more than we care to give; we can anticipate their pushback when we draw healthy boundaries and preplan a response to preempt them.

Finally, just as hostage negotiators work as a team, sometimes we need a team too. As we formulate our response to an anticipated conflict, it's wise to run our thoughts by a godly friend or mentor. An objective opinion will greatly increase our chance of preparing the wisest response. And if our efforts at resolving conflict don't work out as we hoped, we won't second-guess how we handled ourselves and hang our heads in regret.

Everyone has idiosyncrasies. Everyone has expectations. Everyone faces conflict. This is reality. When we know how to respond in our real-life, crazy, expectation-filled relationships, we can stop many conflicts before they start and defuse other conflicts before they get worse.

Lord, I desperately want less conflict in my life. Please help me give grace to my loved ones' idiosyncrasies and own my triggers too. Show me where my expectations have not been realistic. Point out how I have tried to communicate my wants, needs, and expectations in a way that's been unclear or unkind. Give me Your wisdom to plan a godly response for relationships that always seem to go south. Thank You for doing all these things and more. Help me be attuned to Your voice, amen.

PUTTING PEACE INTO PRACTICE

1. Remember what JP said: "Expectation without communication leads to frustration." Is there an issue that repeatedly frustrates you? Is the source of your frustration an unmet expectation? If so, what is the expectation? Write it out. Often seeing our expectation in black and white helps us evaluate whether the expectation is reasonable and realistic.

2. Have you communicated your expectation to the appropriate person clearly and kindly? If not, write down what you will say. (Remember, "I'd like" or "I'd prefer" is often better received than "I expect" when communicating peer to peer.)

3. Can you identify a trigger in yourself? In someone close to you? How have you dealt with this trigger in the past? What do you think is the best way to handle it in the future?

4. Is there any person for whom you should develop a plan so their issue doesn't take you hostage? Prayerfully consider this relationship. Seek wise counsel if necessary.

TWELVE

THE HEALING POWER
OF FORGIVENESS

That relationship. Yeah, *that* one. When you began the relationship, you didn't sign up for heartache or headaches, did you?

Oh sure, you know conflict is part of life. Everyone knows. What you didn't know then was how deeply the spouse, child, friend, neighbor, or coworker would wound you.

But here you are. The conflict happened. Or is happening.

The hurt is real. So is the anger. And the confusion. You wish it all could just vanish in a *poof!* or that you could magically start from the beginning, preventing the hurtful words and actions from happening in the first place.

Even when we are in loving, healthy relationships, conflict is inevitable. If we're dancing with dysfunction, the magnitude of conflict is multiplied. Since we are human, the potential to hurt one another in the midst of conflict is real.

Enter the need for forgiveness.

What is forgiveness, exactly? Why should we forgive? How

should we forgive? These are the questions on the table. Entire books have been written about forgiveness, but in this chapter, we'll touch on the most necessary components of forgiveness so we can work through conflict in a healthy way.

Forgiveness is at the heart of the gospel. Just as our relationship with God depends on His forgiveness of our sins, our relationship with others hinges on our forgiveness of them and their forgiveness of us.

Jesus taught us to pray: "Forgive us our sins, as we have forgiven those who sin against us" (Matthew 6:12 NLT). In Colossians 3:13 we're instructed to "[bear] with one another and, if one has a complaint against another, [forgive] each other; as the Lord has forgiven you, so you also must forgive" (ESV).

Forgiveness is a hallmark of a believer's life.

But that doesn't mean it's always easy.

During the months after my "some days I feel like I want to burn down the church" episode, I struggled with forgiveness. I knew Jesus commanded me to forgive as I had been forgiven, but I wrestled with *how* to forgive. Frankly, my heart felt like someone had taken a giant sledgehammer and shattered it into a million pieces. I often found myself wondering, *How does a fractured person extend forgiveness?* Forgiveness felt foreign.

One evening I tiptoed my way into vulnerability and shared my private struggle with the worship pastor's wife from our former church.

"I know God tells me to forgive, and I *want* to forgive because I know I should. But I don't know how. I don't know if I can."

My confession revealed guilt and shame layered like globs of icky, black tar on my broken heart.

She placed her gentle hands on my shoulders, turned me to face her, eye to eye, and looked at me with complete compassion.

"I want you to listen to me. The fact that you *want* to learn to forgive pleases God. In time, He'll show you how."

In that moment, my guilt and shame melted, and the process of healing forgiveness began.

The first step to forgiving is wanting to learn how—if only because God says we should.

But perhaps you're in a place where your wounds are so deep you don't want to forgive. Maybe the idea of forgiveness seems unfair. Possibly the thought of forgiveness makes you mad.

May I gently place my hand on your shoulders and whisper something to you? *Pray for the "want to."* Start there.

After years of working through forgiveness, here's what I know: forgiveness is a command, forgiveness is a choice, and forgiveness is a process.

FORGIVENESS IS A COMMAND

Forgiveness has always been a messy, confusing issue. So much so that two thousand years ago, Peter, one of Jesus' twelve apostles, asked Jesus a point-blank question about forgiveness: "Lord, how many times shall I forgive my brother or sister who sins against me? Up to seven times?" (Matthew 18:21). I'm certain Peter considered forgiving someone seven times generous. He may have even thought Jesus would be impressed with his willingness to grant forgiveness repeatedly.

Jesus responded: "I tell you, not seven times, but seventy-seven times" (Matthew 18:22).

The point Jesus was making, of course, is that we forgive *whenever* someone sins against us and asks for forgiveness. There's no "Oops, you reached your forgiveness limit" in the kingdom of God.

It's important to note the context here. Right before Peter asked Jesus how many times we should forgive, Jesus had given these instructions: "If your brother or sister sins, go and point out their fault, just between the two of you. If they listen to you, you have won them over" (Matthew 18:15). We looked at this command in depth in an earlier chapter and discussed the importance of addressing an offense quickly and privately. It's easiest to forgive when there aren't layers of unaddressed wrongs piled up like a mound of garbage. Then, after Jesus answered "seventy times seven," He told the story of the unmerciful servant who had been forgiven a large debt but refused to offer forgiveness to someone who owed him a small debt. Jesus' instruction about forgiveness was sandwiched between two narratives that discussed conflict and what to do in the midst of it.

God forgave our (huge!) debt of sin against Him when Jesus offered Himself as the payment for our sin on the cross. Because we are the recipients of undeserved forgiveness, we also ought to be extenders of undeserved forgiveness.

Embedded in Jesus' teaching is this crucial fact: everyone needs forgiveness for something, sometime.

That means me. That means you.

UNFORGIVENESS IS THE FATAL FLAW THAT WILL FRACTURE A RELATIONSHIP BEYOND REPAIR.

Conflicts cannot be resolved without forgiveness, and relationships cannot be sustained without forgiveness. Unforgiveness is the fatal flaw that will fracture a relationship beyond repair.

Perhaps this is one of several reasons forgiveness is a command.

FORGIVENESS IS A CHOICE

While forgiveness is a command, the act of forgiveness is a choice. We forgive with our will, but the process of forgiveness takes place in our hearts.

Biblically, to forgive means "to let go." When we choose to forgive, we let go of our right to get even and we allow God to take over. We let go of our bitterness. We let go of our resentment. We let go of our propensity to bring up the past as an ongoing assault of guilt and shame.

It's been said that "unforgiveness is like drinking poison and hoping the other person dies." If we refuse to forgive, we eventually become bitter, resentful, self-righteous, or spiteful people. Ironically, our perpetrator pays no price for the poison in our soul. However, when unforgiveness reigns unfettered, our joy, contentment, and usefulness to God die slow, painful deaths. The conflict we wish would go away lives on in our hearts, minds, and souls.

As long as we cling to unforgiveness, we remain chained to past hurt. We live enslaved, revisiting the incident in our minds over and over, wondering how to unshackle the chain.

The choice to forgive loosens the chain and sets us free.

However, the choice to forgive will feel difficult—maybe even impossible—if we falsely believe (1) that forgiveness means offering the offender a free pass to hurt us again or (2) that forgiveness means saying, "What you did to me was no big deal."

On the contrary: forgiveness means the offense was such a big deal it cost Jesus His life.

Since forgiveness is not giving our offender a free pass to hurt us again, the choice to forgive shouldn't be equated with the choice to trust or be reconciled. Forgiveness takes one person, but trust and reconciliation take two.

Forgiveness is given. Trust is earned.

Forgiveness can be immediate. Trust takes time.

Forgiveness keeps no record of wrongs. Reconciliation requires ownership and repentance.

Making the choice to forgive is an act of obedience that sets us free, sets the stage for healing all parties, and sets us on the path to genuinely experience the gospel in living color.

FORGIVENESS IS A PROCESS

There is no one-size-fits-all design for forgiveness. Sometimes the choice to forgive is all that's required for us to move forward in a relationship. Other times forgiveness is multilayered. If a wound merely scratches our emotional surface, the process of forgiveness can be quick. However, when a wound cuts deep, the process of forgiveness takes more time.

In some cases, we may need to choose to forgive at eight in the morning and choose to forgive the same offense at nine! If this is you—if you make the choice to forgive but feel the feelings generated by unforgiveness ten minutes later—you need to know you're not alone. You're not a bad Christian. You're simply a person in process.

I've found that inviting Jesus into the process of forgiveness makes everything easier. After all, Jesus is the Master Forgiver. What's more, Jesus understands betrayal, heartache, rejection, being misunderstood, physical abuse, abandonment, being despised, and false accusations, just to name a few. Our Savior is called "a man of sorrows . . . acquainted with grief" (Isaiah 53:3 ESV). Hebrews 4:15 also tells us Jesus understands and empathizes with our human condition. You can simply say, "Jesus, I invite You into my heartache."

When we invite Jesus into our pain and ask Him to help us to forgive, Jesus doesn't shame; Jesus sympathizes. He leans toward us, wraps His loving arms around us, and tenderly whispers, "I know. I've felt it too. I understand, and I can help."

If you find yourself struggling with the forgiveness process, picture your hand in a clenched fist. Better yet, make a fist right now. Envision the issue that wounded you—the one you know you need to forgive but can't quite find it in your heart to do so—inside your tightly held fingers, resting on your palm. Each finger represents a reason you haven't let go: it wasn't fair; they got away with it; they skipped off to a new life, leaving you with their baggage; you want them to feel as badly as you do; they sinned while you tried not to; they need to make it right; you want them to pay for what they did; they shouldn't have said what they said or did what they did; they treated you wrong. The list could go on.

Now, gently unfurl each finger, one by one, until the core offense lays bare.

Turn your hand over and drop the offense into the nail-scarred hands of Jesus.

That's forgiveness.

It's important to give yourself grace as you navigate the process of forgiveness, but don't throw up your hands in despair and stop choosing to forgive, even if it takes time. Remember, forgiveness is both a choice and a process. If you follow God's ways, if you invite Him into your hurt, and if you keep making the choice to forgive, one day you'll wake up with the realization that unforgiveness no longer has a hold on you. The process of forgiveness will have morphed into actual forgiveness.

And you'll be free.

If all this isn't sufficient motivation to choose to obey Christ's command to forgive, remember: as long as you harbor unforgiveness in your heart, you'll remain hurt.

What do hurt people do? Hurt people hurt people.

You won't be the exception.

Oh, you may not hurt people intentionally, but you'll hurt them by building walls that keep them from really knowing you and loving you. You'll be suspicious. You'll be insecure. You'll be controlling. You'll cling too tightly. You'll assume the worst about others and become judge and jury in all your relationships. As a result, conflict will continue to follow you wherever you go. You'll wonder why your relationships seem to have more conflict than other people's relationships.

Yes, making the choice to forgive can be difficult, and yes, the process can be long. But the price we pay for living with unforgiveness is too high not to forgive.

WHEN YOU'RE THE ONE WHO NEEDS TO BE FORGIVEN

Forgiveness is a two-way street. Sometimes we'll need to forgive; other times we'll need to be forgiven. This will be the case until heaven. It shouldn't shock us; Jesus knew sin, hurt, betrayal, and pain would plague the human race long after His death and resurrection, so He gave His followers specific instructions: "Therefore, if you are offering your gift at the altar and there remember that your brother or sister has something against you, leave your gift there in front of the altar. First go and be reconciled to them; then come and offer your gift" (Matthew 5:23–24).

Jesus places relational reconciliation over worship and service to God! We can't authentically worship or offer pure service if we've knowingly wronged someone but haven't made it right. (Think about that the next time you're in church or a Bible study but have treated someone wrongly. Wow!)

Paul echoed this admonition when he wrote, "If it is possible, as far as it depends on you, live at peace with everyone" (Romans 12:18). It's the "as far as it depends on you" part we need to own. We can't be responsible for other people's behavior, but we are responsible for ours.

Frankly, some of us have ignored this clear command. We've offered a weak attempt at making things right, but we haven't gone far; certainly not "as far as it depends on [us]." We've put off the apology we know we need to give. We haven't paid for something we damaged. We've excused our behavior. We've avoided the conversation. And in doing so, we've allowed a conflict to continue in the other person's heart, if not our own.

> WE CAN'T BE RESPONSIBLE FOR OTHER PEOPLE'S BEHAVIOR, BUT WE ARE RESPONSIBLE FOR OURS.

We haven't left our gifts at the altar and made a beeline for a brother or sister toward whom we've behaved badly.

I know. I know. I'm cringing too.

Making things right starts with ownership. Ownership expresses itself in apology.

A sincere apology includes five essential components: taking responsibility, expressing regret, making amends, owning your part but not theirs, and letting go of expectations. Omit any of the five, and reconciliation will be unlikely.

1. TAKE RESPONSIBILITY

A sincere apology must start with personal responsibility for any wrong done, without defending behavior or projecting blame. Statements like "I'm sorry *you* took what I said the wrong way" or "I'm sorry I criticized you, *but*..." put the responsibility (and blame) on the other person. These types of apologies will be perceived as half-hearted at best.

"Apologies" where we defend our behavior with "But you..." or "I'm sorry you..." are backhanded ways of pretending to be sorry for our actions when, in fact, we aren't. In contrast, "I'm sorry my words hurt your feelings. I was harsh and shouldn't have spoken to you that way" puts the ownership—and responsibility—on us.

To simplify, an apology that starts with "I'm sorry *you*..." or "I'm sorry *but*..." won't mend a relationship; an apology that starts with "I'm sorry *I*..." has the potential for relational healing.

2. EXPRESS REGRET

Expressing regret means identifying with the hurt we caused another person. The other person feels bad about what happened; they'd like to know we genuinely feel bad about making them feel bad. Relational hurt must be acknowledged before relational healing can happen.

If we miss this, we miss the whole point.

Making jokes, minimizing wrongs, or sweeping hurtful words or actions under the rug in hopes they'll be forgotten can never heal a broken heart or repair a fractured relationship. Expressing regret is often the most powerful component of an apology, especially when our apology is offered to someone with whom we're in close relationship, like a family member or friend.

A coworker recently shared how her eighty-year-old mother pulled her aside to say she knew she hadn't been a good mother. The mother expressed regret over the way her words and actions hurt my coworker during her childhood. This confession of real regret was the catalyst that began healing their relationship, which had been strained for over fifty years.

3. MAKE AMENDS

Making amends is necessary in some instances, like when property has been destroyed or trust has been broken. Years ago, my husband walked to his car one Sunday after church and noticed a note on his windshield. This is what it said:

> Dear Pastor JP,
>
> I accidentally hit your car while backing out. You'll notice a dent in the bumper. I'm so sorry! But we're brothers in Christ, so you're commanded to forgive me (ha ha!).
>
> Sorry again.

The perpetrator didn't sign his name, making this note the best example of a non-apology apology I've ever seen.

Rather than taking ownership of wrong done, the offender left us with the financial responsibility of fixing something he damaged. Making amends means doing whatever it takes to fix whatever we broke—be it materially, emotionally, relationally, or spiritually. "I intend to pay for the repairs" or "What can I do to regain your trust?" are responses that show the sincerity of our intent. Of course, we must follow through with our commitment to make things right. If we don't, the relationship will likely wind up destroyed beyond repair.

4. OWN YOUR PART, NOT THEIR PART

The fourth component of a healthy apology involves taking ownership of our part in the conflict, without taking ownership of the other person's part. Many people hesitate to apologize because they mistakenly believe that an apology suggests they are at fault for the entirety of the problem. It's important to own whatever part we played in the conflict, while also refusing to take the blame for parts of the conflict we didn't cause.

Some people struggle with apologies not because they don't own their part but because they own their part *on steroids*. These folks over-apologize. Their sense of guilt and shame over wrongs they've done clings to their conscience like cigarette smoke clings to curtains. A healthy apology means we admit guilt, ask for forgiveness, and move forward in freedom.

It bears mentioning that when God tells us to live at peace with all people as far as it depends on us, He's acknowledging that in some instances we'll do our best to make peace, but the other person won't allow it.

They won't accept our apology. They won't forgive us. They'll leave us, reject us, or keep us at arm's length.

This will hurt. It *will*.

But if we can honestly say we did everything we knew to do to make things right, we don't have to hang our heads in regret, guilt, or shame. We can let it go. Sometimes, we let them go.

5. LET GO OF EXPECTATIONS

Finally, a sincere apology is given with no strings attached.

During college I grew in my faith and became aware of the role an apology plays in relational peace, personal peace, and spiritual peace. One weekend I was home from school and got into a silly argument with my younger sister. Feeling convicted about my part of the conflict, I walked into her bedroom to apologize.

"Well, I'm glad you're sorry because this whole thing was completely your fault. I'm not sure I forgive you," my sister shot back.

Her words surprised me and stung. I left her room, sulking. From my vantage point, the conflict had most definitely *not* been all my fault.

Back in my own bedroom, I stewed over her response to my apology. The expectation I had placed on how I thought our interaction would play out versus how it did play out made me mad. I marched back into her room.

"I take back my apology. I'm not sorry. *At all!*" I stomped out of her room and slammed the door for dramatic effect.

Obviously, I had a *long* way to go in learning about healthy, heartfelt apologies!

My sister and I laugh over this silly incident now. All is forgiven.

However, it's important to note that when we apologize, the other person may not respond in a way we'd like them to respond. But, like all things relational, their actions are their responsibility; our actions are our responsibility.

As long as we have relationships, we'll need to forgive and to be forgiven. It's been said that "the first to apologize is the bravest, the first to forgive is the strongest, and the first to forget is the happiest." God's relationship with us—where He freely forgives not just seventy times seven but seventy times seventy and more—is the model for our human relationships. Forgiveness is a command, a choice, and a process that loosens the chains that bind us—setting us free to love and be loved as God intended.

God, thank You for forgiving me. Although I didn't deserve it, You not only forgave all the wrongs I've committed against

You and others, but You also paid for those sins on the cross. Because of the blood of Christ, I don't have a single sin that You have not forgiven. Not one. When I pause to consider the gravity of Your forgiveness, I'm awestruck by Your grace. Father, as an act of obedience, and out of gratitude for what You've done for me, I choose to forgive the person who wronged me. I release my desire to get even, and I respond with my desire for You to be glorified. Help me and heal me through the process of forgiveness. I pray this in Jesus' name and because of His blood, amen.

PUTTING PEACE INTO PRACTICE

1. Is there anyone you need to forgive? If so, whom? Pause right now and tell God you are making the choice to forgive. It's important to note that the feelings of forgiveness may not come immediately. Remember, forgiveness is both a choice that begins with the will and a process that bears fruit in the heart. If you aren't in a place where you want to forgive, start by asking God to give you the "want to." This, too, is an act of obedience.

2. How would you explain the difference between forgiveness and trust? Between forgiveness and reconciliation?

3. Is there anyone you need to ask for forgiveness? If so, decide when and how you will apologize using the five components of a healthy apology.

THIRTEEN

HOW TO DISAGREE WITHOUT BEING DISAGREEABLE (AND HOW TO SPOT THOSE WHO CAN'T)

One of my daughters was on a high school sports team with a gal who could best be described as a "mean girl." To complicate matters, the mean girl presented herself as an angel to teachers and parents; only her peers knew the truth. The never-ending stream of drama, conflict, and confusion the teammate generated would have exhausted an adult, but it proved excruciating for my sixteen-year-old daughter.

At first my daughter tried to talk things through, but she soon learned addressing issues only compounded the problem. I counseled my daughter to take the high road, despite how others behaved. We role-played scenarios at home and practiced how to respond wisely to the constant conflict and resulting headaches, heartaches, and hurt the mean girl instigated. We spent hours praying. Finally, it became clear that despite all my daughter's best efforts, conflict was here to stay.

My Southern relatives call some people *pot stirrers*. The term always makes me smile, even though the fallout from dealing with pot stirrers is no laughing matter. *Pot stirrer* is an apt description for people who love to keep conflict going—folks who stir up drama in places it wouldn't otherwise exist.

Sometimes you can't stop a pot stirrer from stirring the pot.

POT STIRRERS

A pot stirrer says things like this:

- "You weren't bothered by that comment? You must be a lot nicer than me."
- "I'm not gossiping, but . . ."
- "You know me. I'm not one to create drama. However . . ."
- "I probably shouldn't tell you what so-and-so said, but . . ."

Comments like these stir up conflict in relationships that, until the pot was stirred, were cooking just fine on their own.

Pot stirrers often triangulate relationships. They're the third wheel—a go-between for two people who should be talking directly, who almost always prolong a conflict. Pot stirrers find significance in being "in the know." They'll often spark controversy online or on social media. Sometimes pot stirrers are driven by jealousy; often they're motivated by insecurity. Pot stirrers feed on drama, so for them, conflict resolution is water on a grease fire. They may say they want peace, but their words and actions communicate otherwise.

A pot stirrer cannot disagree without being disagreeable. This doesn't mean they don't present themselves as nice people; often they're masters at appearing sweet, kind, or "concerned." However, drama is so ingrained in their way of life that they have a hard time functioning without disagreements. Be forewarned, a pot stirrer spells "concern" *c-h-a-o-s.*

LIFE DRAINERS

Pot stirrers aren't the only ones who can't disagree without being disagreeable. One of my friends likes to use the term *life drainers* for people who aren't concerned about conflict resolution or relationship reconciliation, but whose primary intention is to prove they are right. They drain joy and peace because we engage with them—often for days, weeks, or months—in the hopes of finding unity, solutions, or understanding, only to discover they aren't interested in these things at all. They leave us emotionally, relationally, and spiritually spent.

Life drainers say things like "I don't think wrong things; therefore, the way I see this issue is right." (I actually heard someone say this once.) Even if a life drainer doesn't come right out and verbalize this belief, they think it.

Life drainers are often critical and controlling. They see compromise as a last resort (if they consider compromise at all) since their goal is to prove they know best. Relationships are secondary. Listening to another's perspective is a waste of time for them. After all, why listen to someone else when you're certain your way is the only way? They'd much prefer—in fact, they often demand—that you listen to them. Life drainers are starved bulldogs with fresh meat; they bite and simply will not let things go. If a life drainer can't control, a life drainer will find something to criticize and then leave.

Sometimes life drainers are easy to spot; they're contentious from the start. Other times, though, life-draining tendencies lie dormant. You won't know someone is a life drainer so long as you both agree. But the moment you don't see eye to eye—*bam!*—the life drainer won't stop until you admit they are right.

Years ago, a man at a church we attended became disgruntled over a decision the pastoral team made. Instead of seeking first to understand, he called one of the pastors in a huff.

The parishioner was demanding and full of rage from the moment the conversation began: "Did you say such and such in the meeting where you made the decision? Yes or no?"

The pastor stayed calm in the face of unjust anger. "I think if you knew more of the context surrounding the decision, it would help clarify things. Let's meet for coffee so I can explain more fully."

"Just answer the question. Did you say _____? Yes or no? Yes or no?" the man commanded, his voice rising with every word.

"As I mentioned, there is context surrounding what was said that's important to know. We're brothers in Christ. Let's meet for coffee."

"I don't want to meet you. I want you to answer the question: yes or no?"

You probably guessed the disgruntled church member was more interested in proving his point than in maintaining unity. You probably also guessed that he left the church.

Life drainers are not always aggressive though. Sometimes life drainers suck the joy out of relationships using more passive means.

For example, consider Emily and Pam. They were the best of friends.

Until they weren't.

Without warning, Emily stopped returning Pam's calls or texts. Pam left voice mail messages and countless texts asking Emily what she'd done wrong. She apologized for anything she might have said or done, though she honestly had no idea what might have offended her friend to the point of being completely cut off.

Desperate to resolve whatever conflict had come between them, Pam knocked on Emily's door unannounced.

"Emily, you're my dear friend. Please tell me what I did. I want to make this right," Pam pleaded.

"You should know what you did. If you don't know, I'm not going to tell you," Emily said dryly before shutting the door, leaving Pam standing alone on the porch.

Pam left heartbroken.

And Pam remained heartbroken, pierced by rejection until a wise friend gave her godly advice: "Some people want to hold on to their grudge more than they want to hold on to their relationship. If you sincerely did all you could to reconcile, and yet the other person doesn't want to, move on. You did what is right before God. That's your only responsibility."

No matter what you dub them—pot stirrers, life drainers, or some other name of your own making—these folks haven't grasped how to disagree without being disagreeable. Yet it's vital to take a good look in the mirror. An honest assessment might reveal that *we* can be the pot stirrer. *We* may be the life drainer.

If we find that drama seems to follow us wherever we go, or if we find ourselves constantly irritated at others, we likely need to make some changes. We don't *have* to be a pot stirrer. We don't *have* to be a life drainer. We can learn new, healthier, holier ways of handling disagreements.

And we don't we have to allow pot-stirring,

WE CAN LEARN NEW, HEALTHIER, HOLIER WAYS OF HANDLING DISAGREEMENTS.

life-draining folks to control our lives with their incessant need to bring chaos into our calm. We can disagree without being disagreeable.

Of course, the natural question is how.

And, as always, the answer is found by looking at Jesus.

JESUS, THE LIFE GIVER

In Jesus' day the Pharisees were the ultimate pot stirrers. And life drainers. Everywhere Jesus went the Pharisees challenged Him, attempted to stir up the crowd against Him, or some combination of both. If a group of Pharisees was present, conflict was not far behind.

How did Jesus respond to an almost constant barrage of opposition? Jesus was never unkind or unloving. However, Jesus didn't have an insatiable need for everyone to like Him, which freed Him to seek to please the Father above all else. When confronted with conflict, more often than not Jesus calmly spoke truth and left it at that.

Jesus did not over-engage with people who had no real interest in finding peace and reconciliation. But Jesus didn't under-engage with them either.

Jesus depended on His relationship with the Father to know when to speak, when to remain silent, when to stay, when to leave, and when to graciously let others leave.

We can do the same.

Conflict can drive us to the foot of the cross. It can provide an opportunity for us to live in dependence on our heavenly Father, who promises to give wisdom to those who ask. Instead of relying on resolution strategies (which have their place), sometimes conflict forces us to rely on our resurrected Savior. God knows when we should keep trying and when we should quit. He knows when it's wise to walk away and when it's wise to run.

As a general rule, though, if a person constantly dredges up drama, it's usually best to keep them at arm's length. And if a person is consistently more interested in proving their point than improving your relationship, it's usually wisest to love them from a distance. These types of people have no real interest in unity, conflict resolution, or relational reconciliation.

To handle conflict like Jesus, we do our part to be at peace with all people—while also acknowledging that not everyone will want to be at peace with us.

HOW TO DISAGREE WITHOUT BEING DISAGREEABLE

The Johnsons are conservative Republicans, and the Millers are liberal Democrats. For years they gave each other no more than polite nods, but now they serve on a committee together. Neither couple wants to offend the other, but neither do they want to back down from their convictions. How can they dialogue without being demeaning? How can they debate without being destructive?

Political difference is just one example where the need to disagree without being disagreeable is real. All of us face myriad scenarios with a multitude of diverging opinions every week, sometimes every day. How can any of us disagree without being disagreeable?

To answer that question, let's circle back to some of the principles we learned in previous chapters. I've condensed the most important components of handling conflict into six simple points.

1. MAINTAIN AN ATTITUDE OF HUMILITY

A disagreement centers around an issue; being disagreeable centers around an attitude. If we're prideful, condescending, self-focused, full of rage, or unwilling to listen, conflict has little chance (dare I say *no chance?*) of being handled in a Christ-honoring way. Humility requires us to take the log out of our own eye before taking the speck out of another's eye and to examine how we might have contributed to the conflict, even unintentionally. Humility means we view conflict through the lens of "me and you" rather than "me versus you."

The most powerful prayer we can pray during conflict is "Lord, help me choose to be humble here."

2. TALK *TO* THE PERSON, NOT *ABOUT* THE PERSON

If we talk *to* the person rather than *about* the person, little conflicts don't become huge conflicts. When we address an issue rather than attack or avoid a person, we build bridges instead of walls. We choose the time and place to address the disagreement carefully; no one handles conflict well when they're tired, stressed, sick, or hungry. It can be helpful to ask, "I'd like to talk about this particular issue. Is this a good time for you?"

Then we think about what we're going to say before we say it. We can write a script for high-stakes relationships or high-tension topics. A script allows us to evaluate our words and edit if necessary. Remembering the Golden Rule is essential to determining what to say and how to say it. We can ask ourselves: *How would I want this subject to be broached if a person needed to address this issue with me?*

3. AFFIRM THE RELATIONSHIP

Maybe you've noticed the same thing I've noticed: that it's difficult to be disagreeable when I'm affirming a relationship. Sincere statements like "I value our friendship," "You are an important part of this management team," "I want the best for you," and "I love you and want us to work this out" have a way of disarming defenses and disagreeable attitudes (both ours and theirs) from the start.

It's also helpful to affirm common interests or concerns up front so conversations begin with two parties on the same page, even if they have differing perspectives or opinions. Phrases like "I know we both want to solve this problem" or "This is probably as frustrating for you as it is for me" position us to address conflict from the perspective of "me and you" rather than "me against you."

4. LEAD WITH LISTENING

When we listen before we launch into our concerns or complaints, we gain insight we wouldn't otherwise have. By asking open-ended questions like "What happened?" "What's your perspective?" and "What's your main concern?" we gain a more complete picture of the issue at hand and the other person's driving motivations. With a broader view, we can better discern real issues versus surface issues.

Listening also pumps the brakes on our propensity to create a narrative in our minds where we're the sinless victim and the other person is the sinful villain. And listening does one more important thing—an essential thing, actually: listening communicates care. People open up when they feel cared for. People clam up or power up when they feel controlled.

5. ADDRESS ONE ISSUE AT A TIME

When we keep short accounts with our friends, family members, and coworkers, we talk about conflict and concerns sooner rather than later—on the same day, if possible. This way, issues don't build up, which means tempers are less likely to flare. We clearly address the issue at hand; we don't drop hints like bread crumbs and hope the other person will guess what's wrong. We don't dump several issues into the equation either; instead we address one issue at a time.

> ISSUES DON'T BUILD UP, WHICH MEANS TEMPERS ARE LESS LIKELY TO FLARE.

As we address the offense or state our opinion, we speak calmly and respectfully. We keep the problem the problem and resist the temptation to make the person the problem.

6. MOVE FORWARD INTO DEEPER INTIMACY OR MOVE ON WITH DEEPER INSIGHT

When conflict is handled according to God's blueprint, the likelihood of a positive resolution is greatly increased. A disagreement that once stood as a barrier between two people is removed. And, because they worked together to work through conflict, greater intimacy is possible and greater respect is likely. Destructive walls are replaced with constructive ways of relating.

However, as we discussed at the beginning of this chapter, sometimes walls don't come down, though not from lack of effort. We move on when a conflict can't be resolved, but we do so with deeper insight into our relationship with God and our relationship with others and even deeper insight into ourselves. Every conflict is an opportunity to learn something.

SUMMING IT UP

Few of us enjoy conflict, but it's possible to disagree without being disagreeable. Some conflicts—and some people—make this easier. Some make it harder.

If conflict happens in a way that gives us space to think through our response, we're less likely to be disagreeable. We can think, pray, and prepare the way we broach the topic, using the six conflict principles listed previously as our guide.

However, real life happens in real time. Many conflicts, maybe *most* conflicts, take us by surprise. In these instances, we typically have knee-jerk reactions to hurt and anger. But the more we practice the six major principles of conflict management, the more we'll gravitate toward implementing them, even when we're sucker punched by disagreements. Over time, our knee-jerk reactions will become need-based responses. We'll be people who can disagree without being disagreeable.

Father, I know disagreements are part of life, so teach me to disagree without being disagreeable. Show me where I'm not humble. Remind me to listen, to affirm, and to speak respectfully as I discuss differences of opinion, differences of priorities, and differences of perspective. Help me not "stir the pot" and create unnecessary drama. Help me be a life giver, not a life drainer, amen.

PUTTING PEACE INTO PRACTICE

1. Do you see any "pot stirrer" tendencies in yourself? Do you see any "life drainer" tendencies? If yes, what will you do to put these habits aside and learn to disagree without being disagreeable?

2. Review the six conflict resolution principles, listed below. Circle the one you need to practice the most. Underline principles you already practice on a consistent basis.

   1) Maintain an Attitude of Humility
   2) Talk *to* the Person, Not *About* the Person
   3) Affirm the Relationship
   4) Lead with Listening
   5) Address One Issue at a Time
   6) Move Forward into Deeper Intimacy or Move On with Deeper Insight

3. Consider a recent conflict. Using the six principles as your guide, write out a plan for addressing the disagreement without being disagreeable.

FOURTEEN

YOU'VE DONE THE RIGHT THING; DON'T DO THE WRONG THING NOW

True confession: the title of this chapter is a note I wrote to myself in a season of navigating prolonged conflict. If you and I are ever together, you can ask to see it; I keep it in the notes of my cell phone. The day I typed these words, I knew they'd come straight from the hand of God.

You've done the right thing; don't do the wrong thing now.

In the previous thirteen chapters we've explored why conflict comes calling and what to do when it does. We've learned to focus on changing ourselves rather than changing someone else. We've discussed best practices, examined Scripture, and learned conflict resolution strategies. Hopefully, as we've faced conflict, we've chosen to do the right thing—and if we haven't, we've chosen to make things right.

However, prolonged conflict has a way of wearing us down. When we're weary, we can easily lose our way. And our patience. And our self-control. And our good sense. It can happen to anyone.

Remember Moses? The great man of God who led the Israelites out of Egypt, parted the Red Sea, received the Ten Commandments, and guided God's people through the wilderness to the edge of the promised land? Moses became so exasperated with the constant complaints and conflict he endured from the Israelites he disobeyed God's clear command and struck a rock in anger. This act of disobedience kept Moses from entering the promised land.

Moses' promised land was a physical one, but our disobedience to God's instructions regarding anger can keep us out of our relational promised land—the promised land of peace, unity, and favor God longs to bestow on His children. Which is why, in the heat of battle, we need to remind ourselves not to do the wrong thing now that we've come this far in doing the right thing.

WHY IS DOING THE RIGHT THING SO HARD SOMETIMES?

If you're reading this book, I know something about you: you don't want to handle conflict the wrong way. You, my friend, *want* to do right. If your heart was bent on handling hurt, anger, misunderstanding, and relational drama any way you please, you would have put this book aside pages ago. But you didn't. You are still here. You're still reading. Still learning. Still praying.

Why, then, is it so hard for us who *want* to do right to actually *do* right when tempers flare, tensions mount, and our tender hearts get torn by conflict?

I read something in the Bible this morning I've read hundreds of times, but today the words leapt off the page. Five words explained why doing right isn't always easy.

The context of these five words is found in 1 Peter 2:9–11:

You are a chosen people, a royal priesthood, a holy nation, God's special possession, that you may declare the praises of him who called you out of darkness into his wonderful light. Once you were not a people, but now you are the people of God; once you had not received mercy, but now you have received mercy. Dear friends, I urge you, as foreigners and exiles, to abstain from sinful desires, which *wage war against your soul.* (emphasis added)

Most read the words *sinful desires* and think of moral or sexual sin. But our sinful desires include relational sins too: our desires to be selfish and self-focused, to respond with pride, to be dismissive of others' concerns, to be short-tempered and impatient, to get even, to avoid issues, to run away from problems, to gossip, to slander, to criticize, to manipulate, to remain bitter, to be controlling, to be hateful, to be spiteful and harsh. Of course, most of us would never want these actions to be true of us. But when we feel mad, or sad, or bad, they oftentimes are. Because—and here's where the five words come into play—our fleshly desires *wage war against our souls.*

Conflict. Is. Battle.

And the biggest battle we face is not with another person or another group of people. Our greatest battle is with ourselves.

Conflict isn't just an external battle; conflict is also an internal battle.

In fact, I'd go so far as to say conflict *starts* as an internal battle, then becomes an external battle.

Since we've been together for fourteen chapters

CONFLICT ISN'T JUST AN EXTERNAL BATTLE; CONFLICT IS ALSO AN INTERNAL BATTLE.

now, may I tell you something I love about this passage from 1 Peter? These scriptures were written by the apostle Peter—the guy who cut off a servant's ear when a crowd came out to arrest Jesus the night before His crucifixion. Peter, the disciple who denied knowing Jesus after three years of close friendship. Peter, the loose cannon, the guy with little self-control and an obvious anger issue. Peter, a man who understood all too well how sin can wage war against a soul and how deeply regret can burden us when sin wins the war.

Our flesh is a powerful foe.

It's important to know that Peter's anger, denial, and lack of self-control took place before the cross and Christ's resurrection, and before God poured out the gift of the Holy Spirit. The flesh is still a force to be reckoned with, but now we have the indwelling Spirit of God to help us fight the battle. Galatians 5 explains this more fully:

> You, my brothers and sisters, were called to be free. But do not use your freedom to indulge the flesh; rather, serve one another humbly in love. *For the entire law is fulfilled in keeping this one command: "Love your neighbor as yourself." If you bite and devour each other, watch out or you will be destroyed by each other.* So I say, *walk by the Spirit, and you will not gratify the desires of the flesh. For the flesh desires what is contrary to the Spirit, and the Spirit what is contrary to the flesh. They are in conflict with each other, so that you are not to do whatever you want.* But if you are led by the Spirit, you are not under the law. (vv. 13–18, emphasis added)

We can choose to do right if we depend on the help of the Holy Spirit.

When we yield to God's Spirit, He produces the fruit of "love, joy, peace, patience, kindness, goodness, faithfulness, gentleness, self-control" in our lives (Galatians 5:22–23 ESV). These are the very character traits we need to handle disagreements and dissensions in a healthy, holy way.

However, even when we depend on the Spirit's help, doing the right thing in the midst of conflict doesn't always come without effort. In fact, sometimes we'll have to fight a spiritual battle to do so. But the reward is worth it. No one ever regrets the choice to do right—at least, not in the long run.

Eventually, Peter learned this truth.

Here's what the once short-tempered, shortsighted Peter wrote later in life:

Finally, all of you, be like-minded, be sympathetic, love one another, be compassionate and humble. Do not repay evil with evil or insult with insult. On the contrary, repay evil with blessing, because to this you were called so that you may inherit a blessing. For,

> "Whoever would love life
>   and see good days
> must keep their tongue from evil
>   and their lips from deceitful speech.
> They must turn from evil and do good;
>   they must seek peace and pursue it.
> For the eyes of the Lord are on the righteous
>   and his ears are attentive to their prayer,
> but the face of the Lord is against those who do evil."

Who is going to harm you if you are eager to do good? But even if you should suffer for what is right, you are blessed. "Do not fear their threats; do not be frightened." But in your hearts revere Christ as Lord. (1 Peter 3:8–15)

The simple truth is that hurt *hurts*, which makes it hard to handle in a holy way. When we're angry or we've been misunderstood, mischaracterized, or mishandled, our natural inclination is to respond *in* hurt with the intent *to* hurt. Some of us lash out while others of us check out.

We know this isn't the best way to handle conflict, and between the covers of this book we've explored what to do instead. Now I want to offer one final suggestion.

Do you recall our opening chapter? The one where I shared about the day I wanted to burn down the church because my family had been hurt and my husband was mischaracterized and betrayed?

One winter evening I went into mama-bear mode (except it was more like wife-bear mode). In the privacy of our home I vented, ranted, and did all the usual things women do when they, or those they love, are treated unfairly. Wisely, behind closed doors, JP let me vent. We both knew talking about the issue to outsiders wasn't a Christ-honoring option, and I suppose JP realized I'd explode if I didn't talk to someone about the hurt.

Except that evening, during a particularly emotional rant, I paused to notice JP hadn't joined my venting party. In retrospect, I now realize I possessed the unfortunate talent of turning a *vent* into an *event*.

There's a fine line between expressing feelings (which is healthy) and vomiting feelings (which makes everyone, including us, feel worse). When we express our feelings, we talk openly to the right person in the right way, which makes us more spiritually and emotionally healthy. When we vomit our feelings, we talk negatively to the wrong person or in a toxic way, which makes us more spiritually sick.

Suddenly, in the middle of my emotional vomit, I realized that JP had not only failed to join me this night; JP had *never* joined my party.

And you know what? *That* made me mad.

I wanted him to attend my pitiful "It's not right! It's not fair!" banquet of pain. But he wouldn't.

THERE'S A FINE LINE BETWEEN EXPRESSING FEELINGS AND VOMITING FEELINGS.

"Why don't you ever say anything bad about those people? They treated you horribly!"

"Donna, do you know who can experience the blessing of God?"

"Um . . . not exactly."

JP pulled out his Bible and read me Psalm 15. (You'll want to read it—it's great!) Then he read me 1 Peter 3, part of which we just covered. (If you skipped over it, go back and read it right now.) After reading, JP directed my attention to two verses in particular: "Do not repay evil with evil or insult with insult. On the contrary, repay evil with blessing, because to this you were called so that you may inherit a blessing. . . . In your hearts revere Christ as Lord" (vv. 9, 15).

"Donna," he said, "if Christ is set apart as Lord of our hearts, then Christ is the example we follow. God's instructions for how we handle relationships—even difficult, painful ones—are what we obey. I simply want to choose to do the right thing, even if no one else does."

Then JP said one last thing that turned out to be truer than I could have imagined back then.

"You'll never regret blessing. You'll eventually regret returning evil for evil or insult with insult, but you will never regret blessing."

Since that fateful season of our life, my husband has made it his ongoing practice to bless others no matter what others do to him. Because he led the way in following Jesus' example and God's Word, I've tried my best to do the same. I'd be lying if I said I've done this perfectly. I haven't. In fact, I'd love a few do-overs.

I'd also be misleading you if I told you this is easy.

It's not.

It's often gut-wrenching—hence the battle that wages war against the soul.

The fact remains: hurt hurts. Choosing to do what's right even if others don't isn't guaranteed to take away the pain. It didn't for Jesus; we'll be disappointed if we think it will for us.

No, following God's way doesn't always take away the pain. *But it does take away the regret.*

And it does something more: it keeps us close to Christ, it allows us to be healing agents of peace, and it makes us usable to God. This is the blessing we get for the blessings we give.

Six weeks ago to the day, I stood in the sanctuary of the church I once wanted to burn down. I'd been invited to speak to several hundred women there.

I stepped onto the stage overcome with utter gratitude and humble awe of how God's instructions are always right and His ways are always best. The crucible of pain had refined me in the most beautiful of ways. As I looked over the sea of women, my eyes brimmed with tears that stung my eyes. But this time, they were tears of thankfulness instead of heartache. I felt certain no one in the crowd knew what it had taken for me to get there, or the changes that had taken place in me along the way. Nor could they fully comprehend the depth of the sweet partnership I now enjoy (JP too!) with this church and its people.

Peace, which once felt like a stranger, is now a friend.

I'll close by reminding you of the exhortations I must continually remind myself: *Choose to do right, even if everyone else chooses wrong. You've done the right thing; don't do the wrong thing now.*

God in heaven, may my words, actions, and choices please You here on earth. Help me follow in the footsteps of Jesus and not repay evil with evil. Help me to bless instead. Help me depend on the Holy Spirit to put to death the desires of my flesh. Help me choose to do right even if everyone around me chooses wrong. Oh God, help me to make regret-free choices in the midst of my real-life conflicts! Thank You for the tools You've given me and for the help of Your Spirit. Thank You for loving me, Lord. I love You, too, amen.

PUTTING PEACE INTO PRACTICE

1. What are some of the good choices you've made to handle conflict in a healthy, holy way recently?
2. Were any of these choices inspired by truths you've learned from reading this book? If so, what did you learn and what was the resulting choice?
3. Can you identify ways prolonged periods of conflict have left you weary and susceptible to reactions you'll later regret? If so, how?
4. How can depending on the Holy Spirit help you in your current conflict? Pause right now and ask God for the help of His Spirit. Tell God you'll yield to His leading.
5. Name a specific way you can bless rather than return insult for insult in the midst of conflict.

CONCLUSION

FINDING PEACE WITH GOD

My friend. Yes, *you*. The one reading these words right now.

It's my sincere desire that the content in these pages has given you the wisdom you need to enjoy the relationships you have and those you will have in the future. I pray the book points you to more peace and less regret in all your interactions with others.

But there's one thing I long for you to experience more than peace in your human relationships: I want you to have peace with God.

Maybe you wonder if a thing like peace with God is attainable. According to God, it is. In fact, God Himself made a way.

The truth is, apart from Christ, all of us have a broken relationship with God. Our distance from God is not a result of anything God did; our fractured fellowship is a result of what we've done or what we've failed to do. Our sinful words, thoughts, and actions have marred our peace with God. None of us is immune. Romans 3:23 says, "All have sinned and fall short of the glory of God."

And as much as we'd like to disagree, we can't. In our heart of hearts, we know it's true.

We would have stayed distant from God, too, had it not been for His great love for us. For His great love for *you*.

Romans 5:8 tells us, "While we were still sinners, Christ died for us." Maybe you've heard about Jesus' death on the cross, but you wonder, *What did Christ's death on the cross accomplish, exactly?*

As the mediator between God and humanity, Jesus paid the penalty of our sins when He died on the cross. Christ took on our sins, purchased our forgiveness, and made a way for us to be reconciled with God: "The wages of sin is death, but the gift of God is eternal life in Christ Jesus our Lord" (Romans 6:23). Not only did Christ's death and resurrection open the way for us to experience eternal life, but they also opened the possibility of peace with God. As Romans 5:1 states: "Therefore, since we have been justified through faith, we have peace with God through our Lord Jesus Christ."

The path to peace with God is paved with faith in Jesus: "For [Jesus] himself is our peace . . . And he came and preached peace to you who were far off and peace to those who were near" (Ephesians 2:14, 17 ESV).

Jesus offers peace with God to anyone who would turn from their sin and turn toward Him. God *wants* a relationship with you. The question, though, is this: *Do you want to be reconciled and have a relationship with Him?*

Listen to what the apostle John said: "For God so loved the world that he gave his one and only Son, that whoever believes in him shall not perish but have eternal life. For God did not send his Son into the world to condemn the world, but to save the world through him" (John 3:16–17).

Motivated by His great love, God gave the world His Son.

Motivated by love, God gave His Son for *you*.

The Son *is* our peace, and without a relationship with the Son, we will never find lasting peace.

Peace with God is not something we could earn by our good deeds or being a "good" person; if that were the case, Jesus would have died in vain. Peace with God is a gift God purchased for us through the death and resurrection of Christ. As Ephesians 2:8–9 puts it, "For it is by grace you have been saved, through faith—and this is not from yourselves, it is the gift of God—not by works, so that no one can boast."

Peace with God is available for everyone who wants it—including you. Peace with God is open to all who have faith, to all who believe that Jesus Christ is the way, the truth, and the life.

God *wants* to have a relationship with you. God provided a way for you to have peace with Him, with others, and with yourself. That way is through Jesus.

If you long to experience peace with God and have a relationship with Him, you can invite God into your life right now. Perhaps you'll want to use the prayer I've written here as a springboard for your own prayer.

That said, peace with God is not experienced through a prayer; prayer is simply a way of communicating our desire to have a relationship with God, *to* God. But prayer does express our faith and our belief.

God, I want to have peace with You. I know I have sinned, Lord. I've said and done things that have damaged my relationships with others and broken my relationship with You. Please forgive me, Lord. Thank You for sending Your Son, Jesus, to take on the burden of my sin on the cross. I believe Jesus died for my sins and that He was raised to life on the third day. Thank You for the free gift of reconciliation and salvation. I want a relationship with You now and forever, amen.

———— o ————

If you invited God into your life, you've begun a relationship with Him—one where He will never leave you or forsake you. You'll want to grow in your relationship with God, so join a Bible-believing church where people are loving and Christ is exalted.

Finally, my friend, may God bless you, your relationship with Him, and your relationships with others.

Peacemakers who sow in peace reap a harvest of righteousness.

James 3:18

ACKNOWLEDGMENTS

A book is never written alone. This one is no exception. This book is a labor of love born from a lifetime of learning.

The words *thank you* fall short in expressing my gratitude, respect, and love for my family—my husband, JP Jones, and my children, Taylor, Kylie, and Ashton. We learned this book and we lived this book years before it was written. God equipped us, and now, through this book, He'll equip others. Isn't He good for using imperfect people like us?

Thank you, Becca Jones, for reading the earliest drafts through the lens of your English teacher expertise. Thank you, Tim Healy, for your kind words of encouragement. With each new addition to our family—by marriage or by birth—JP and I smile and say, "one more person to love!"

Team Jones: I love you and I like you. Always have. Always will.

A special thank you to Lysa TerKeurst, Shae Tate Hill, and the women at Proverbs 31 Ministries for championing this book. Without you, this book would likely never have seen the light of day. You are unselfish heroes who use your gifts to help others and advance God's work. I am forever grateful. Truly.

Thank you also to literary agent, Meredith Brock, who gave me the best advice: "The message that needs to be shared is somewhere in what you've already written. Go back, look harder, and you'll find it." Meredith, I heeded your wisdom, and the result is found between these pages. Your advice was gold!

Thank you to the team at HarperCollins Thomas Nelson for bringing this book to life. Kathryn Notestine and Brigitta Nortker refined the content in the most beautiful of ways. I loved your personal notes along with your edits. Knowing the content was helpful, practical, and doable, even to those looking for typos and edits, gave me courage to continue. Two words describe our working relationship: *Pure. Joy.*

A heartfelt thank-you to my church family, Crossline Church. Much of what I wrote I shared with you first. You all are the most encouraging community of believers. I thank God continually for your support and love.

Thank you, Julie Tenwolde, for loving me well, even in my darkest days. Thank you for accepting me as is but holding me to a higher standard so I could look back on conflict without regret. Thank you, Debbie Pelichowski, for your green light in sharing my church hurt story and for your genuine support in doing so.

Finally, thank you, dear reader, for trusting me to help you navigate the headaches and heartaches of conflict through the lens of God's Word. May you continue to enjoy healthy conflict and reap the blessing of a peaceful life.

NOTES

CHAPTER 2: WHY SO MUCH CONFLICT?

1. Ela Chodyniecka et al., "Money can't buy your employees' loyalty," *People & Organization* (blog), McKinsey & Company, March 28, 2022, https://www.mckinsey.com/capabilities/people-and -organizational-performance/our-insights/the-organization-blog /money-cant-buy-your-employees-loyalty.

2. Karolis Kiniulis, "How Many Selfies Are Taken a Day?" *Eksposure* (blog), July 22, 2022, https://www.eksposure.com/selfie-statistics /#:~:text=Around%2093%20million%20selfies%20are%20taken %20each%20day%3B%20however%2C%20the,around%20450 %20selfies%20a%20year.

3. John M. Gottman and Joan DeClaire, *The Relationship Cure: A Five-Step Guide to Strengthening Your Marriage, Family, and Friendships* (New York: Three Rivers Press, 2011), 28.

4. Henry Cloud and John Townsend, *Boundaries: When to Say Yes, When to Say No to Take Control of Your Life* (Grand Rapids, MI: Zondervan, 1992), 33.

CHAPTER 3: BUT FIRST, REMOVE THE LOG

1. Jill Savage, Life on the Edge of Normal email newsletter, October 16, 2021, www.jillsavage.org/subscribe.

2. Katie Shonk, "Conflict-Management Styles: Pitfalls and Best

Practices," *Program on Negotiation* (blog), Harvard Law School, April 6, 2023, https://www.pon.harvard.edu/daily/conflict-resolution /conflict-management-styles-pitfalls-and-best-practices.

CHAPTER 4: THE ONE QUALITY NO RELATIONSHIP CAN SURVIVE WITHOUT

1. Bible Hub, s.v. "tapeinophrosune," accessed July 27, 2023, https://biblehub.com/greek/5012.htm.
2. Eric Barker, *Plays Well with Others* (New York: HarperOne, 2022), 25.

CHAPTER 5: WHY WE GET MAD (AND WHAT TO DO ABOUT IT)

1. Ken Sande, *The Peacemaker: A Biblical Guide to Resolving Personal Conflict*, 3rd ed. (Grand Rapids: Baker Books, 2004), 103–4.

CHAPTER 6: SHOULD I BE MAD? BIG THINGS, SMALL THINGS, AND EVERYTHING IN BETWEEN

1. Bible Hub, s.v. "orgizó," accessed July 27, 2023, https://biblehub.com /greek/3710.htm.
2. Sande, *The Peacemaker*, 234.

CHAPTER 7: IF EVERYONE WOULD ONLY LISTEN TO ME (OR HOW TO MAKE MISUNDERSTANDINGS A THING OF THE PAST)

1. Clay Drinko, Ph.D, "We're Worse at Listening Than We Realize," *Psychology Today*, August 4, 2021, https://www.psychologytoday.com /us/blog/play-your-way-sane/202108/were-worse-listening-we-realize.
2. Jack Zenger and Joseph Folkman, "What Great Listeners Actually Do," *Harvard Business Review*, July 14, 2016, https://hbr.org/2016 /07/what-great-listeners-actually-do.

CHAPTER 8: CONFLICT SHOULDN'T BE A TEAM SPORT

1. Kerry Patterson et al., *Crucial Conversations: Tools for Talking When Stakes Are High*, 2nd ed. (New York: McGraw-Hill, 2012), 22.
2. Patterson et al., *Crucial Conversations*, 4.
3. Bible Hub, s.v. "elegchó," accessed June 12, 2023, https://biblehub.com /greek/1651.htm.

CHAPTER 9: DO WE REALLY HAVE TO DO THIS? NOW?

1. Bible Hub, s.v. "mataiotés," accessed July 27, 2023, https://biblehub
.com/greek/3153.htm.

2. Bible Hub, s.v. "dianoia," accessed June 12, 2023, https://biblehub
.com/greek/1271.htm.

CHAPTER 10: WAYS WE MAKE THINGS WORSE INSTEAD OF BETTER

1. "Three Phases to Avoid During an Argument," Relationship Zen
(blog), May 5, 2019, https://www.relationshipzen.ca/blog/phrases
-to-avoid-during-an-argument.

CHAPTER 11: HOW TO STOP CONFLICT BEFORE IT STARTS

1. "What is a Hostage Negotiator?" *Program on Negotiation* (blog),
Harvard Law School, https://www.pon.harvard.edu/tag/hostage
-negotiator.

ABOUT THE AUTHOR

Donna Jones is a national speaker, church planter, pastor's wife, and self-described "Bible-explainer" who has spoken in twenty-six states and on four continents. A graduate of UCLA with a degree in interpersonal communications, she hosts the weekly *That's Just What I Needed* podcast, is the author of *Seek: A Woman's Guide to Meeting God*, *Taming Your Family Zoo*, the *Get Healthy* Bible study series, and is a contributing author to the devotionals *A Moment to Breathe* and *Arise, Daily*. A contributor to Crosswalk.com, she has had several articles make the "Top Ten of the Year" list and has been on numerous television and radio shows and podcasts, including *Focus on the Family Broadcast* and *Good Day, Dallas*. Donna is passionate about equipping others to know, love, and follow God in their real, everyday lives. She wants to know, love, and follow God this way herself. She and her husband, JP Jones, make their home in Southern California.

COMPEL
Writers Training

COMPEL Writers Training is a faith-based online community from Lysa TerKeurst and Proverbs 31 Ministries. COMPEL was designed to help writers find direction for their work, receive practical training, and discover the motivation to keep going.

We've built COMPEL around three pillars:

- Community with other writers and COMPEL leaders.
- Content that is practical and inspiring.
- Connection with experts in the field and unique publishing opportunities.